The Conquer Kit

The Conquer Kit

A Creative Business Planner
for Women Entrepreneurs

NATALIE MACNEIL

A TarcherPerigee Book

An imprint of Penguin Random House LLC
375 Hudson Street, New York, New York 10014

LIBRARY OF CONGRESS CATALOGING-IN-PUBLICATION DATA
Names: Macneil, Natalie.
Title: The conquer kit : a creative business planner for women entrepreneurs
/ Natalie MacNeil.
Description: New York : Perigee Books, 2015.
Identifiers: LCCN 2015035529 | ISBN 9780399175770 (paperback)
Subjects: LCSH: Businesswomen. | Entrepreneurship. | Strategic planning. |
BISAC: BUSINESS & ECONOMICS / Entrepreneurship.
Classification: LCC HD6054 .M33 2015 | DDC 658.4/012082—dc23

First edition: December 2015
Printed in the United States of America

7 9 10 8 6

Most TarcherPerigee books are available at special quantity discounts for bulk purchases for sales promotions, premiums, fund-raising, or educational use. Special books, or book excerpts, can also be created to fit specific needs. For details, write: SpecialMarkets@penguinrandomhouse.com.

This book is dedicated to every woman fiercely pursuing her dreams and all those who don't have the opportunity to pursue theirs—yet.

Fifty percent of royalties earned from this book will support students at the Conquer Academy that we helped build in Tanzania, through our #PledgeYourProfits initiative.

To learn more, visit shetakesontheworld.com/pledgeyourprofits.

CONTENTS

What you seek is seeking you.

— RUMI

INTRODUCTION

Long ago and far away in history, conquering meant taking things that didn't belong to you, gaining from someone else's loss, probably while wearing an unflattering uniform. Your army seized land, you won a war, and an empire was yours to rule.

While we all love winning and achieving goals, this book is about navigating life and business with creativity, kindness, and a heart-centered compassion. I want you to achieve things that change lives and even change the world.

FOR ME, CONQUERING MEANS RECOGNIZING THE UNIQUE PURPOSE YOU HAVE ON THIS PLANET AND EARNING A LIVING AT IT. IT MEANS SHINING A LIGHT ON WHAT'S IMPORTANT TO YOU AND LEADING BY EXAMPLE. IT'S HAVING THE COURAGE TO FOLLOW YOUR DREAMS AND INSPIRING THE PEOPLE IN YOUR LIFE TO DO THE SAME.

And there are many, many ways you can inspire and affect change. Volunteer. Raise engaged, curious children. Donate to causes you believe in. These are all worthwhile and very, very important. But if you feel truly, deeply passionate about living a fulfilling life on your own terms, the best way to do that is by building your own business and working for yourself.

Now, a disclaimer: Building a business isn't easy. It takes a lot of courage, tenacity, and conviction. Most people never follow through on their ideas. We both know you're cut from a different cloth, Conqueror.

If you stay rooted in your purpose and the contribution only you can make in the world, you will consistently find guidance and support. Doors will open for you, amazing people will come into your life, and you'll magnetize opportunities. That's the power of passion-fueled living and unapologetically marching to the beat of your own drum.

How do I know? I've witnessed these synchronicities again and again as I've built my own company. I was at the airport in Lima, Peru, telling a gentleman about what I do. Suddenly, a woman turned around and said, "Are you Natalie MacNeil?" We were both thousands of miles from our homes, and she happened to have my contact info in her purse, along with a note to reach out to me because she loved my work. Coincidence? You decide.

For me, success is rooted in having a solid plan—a solid plan that works for me + my business + the way I navigate life. When I started, I knew I needed a system and a method, but traditional business plans induced eye rolls and tears of boredom. I also knew there had to be a way to organize these goals in a creative, fun way. I needed a business plan that I actually wanted to look at every day.

The Conquer Kit was born from this desire and I've been using it to map out my annual business plans for several years now. This plan has become a living, breathing partner in my business. I look at my own Conquer Kit every day to keep an eagle-eye view on my business. I use the exercises in this book to plan who to hire and how to measure my opportunities. I'm so much more focused as a result of this plan. The first year I created this process my business revenue actually doubled!

When I started to see these results, I knew I had to share this process with members of the Conquer Club, my year-long business incubator for ambitious entrepreneurs. They loved it as much as I did—and loved the jaw-dropping results even more.

Dr. Heather Paulson, founder of the Paulson Center in Arizona, says, "The Team Hive in *The Conquer Kit* changed the way I view my whole business and strategically plan for growth."

Ashley Leavy, creator of the Love & Light School of Energy Medicine, says,

"The 5×5 Plan in *The Conquer Kit* was the catalyst for more success in my business. I got clarity on how I need to be spending my time in order to grow my business. It's one of the most important tools I've ever used, and I know I'll continue to use it."

And . . . that was it. I knew I needed to make it available to, well, everyone.

I CREATED *THE CONQUER KIT* TO HELP YOU ACHIEVE YOUR DREAMS IN A WAY THAT FEELS FUN, INSPIRING, ORGANIC, GORGEOUS, AND IN ALIGNMENT WITH *YOU.*

Here's a glance at the goodness to come as we work through the eight steps of your very own Conquer Kit:

STEP 1: Get in the Flow

Fulfilling, meaningful success stems from deep within. In this step, you'll take a look at the passion behind your goals and the beautiful bones of your big vision.

STEP 2: Create Fantastic Things for the World (aka Your Products)

What kind of products should you sell? What can you create that will make you feel the happiest and most alive? In this step you will get the powerful perspective you need.

STEP 3: Form the Four Pillars of Success

From your name to your systems to your legal structure and accounting; you'll build a workable, sustainable platform for your business to stand on—brick by brick.

STEP 4: Get Your Mind on Your Money

You'll finish this step feeling *empowered* (instead of crazy stressed) when it comes to your money. We'll dive into your mindset, and all the savvy systems you need to know about: budget sheets, cash flow statements, profit and loss, and more.

STEP 5: Sell Your Soul (aka Heart-Centric Marketing)

Self-promotion doesn't have to feel icky. Seriously. I'll show you how easy (and fun) it can be to create compelling and value-packed content, craft your story, and become a more confident salesperson.

STEP 6: Build an A-Team

When you're on the entrepreneur's adventure, finding the right help is essential. In this step, I'll equip you with the insight, interview tips, and onboarding ideas you need to build your virtual dream team of designers, assistants, web developers, SEO consultants, and more.

STEP 7: Make a Bigger Picture Plan

Boring business planning? Not in this book. This step is all about taking a heart-centered, visual, and way-too-much-fun approach to setting big goals and achieving them. Strategic planning in your business will never be the same again.

STEP 8: Craft Your Conquer Calendar

In this step you will get so organized you can almost taste the awesome outcome, with this month-by-month goal-setting map that puts a timeline on your milestones. It'll keep you focused and moving forward, all year long.

For each exercise, you'll notice an estimated completion time based on the average amount of time people usually spend on the exercise. Feel free to spend as much, or as little, time on each exercise as you'd like. I pass the torch of creative license on to you now, and encourage you to make this process your own.

To complete the exercises in *The Conquer Kit*, I recommend having the following items on hand:

- Pens and markers in your favorite colors

- A glue stick

- A roll of tape

- A little stack of magazines you love

- Anything else you can think of that will help you make *The Conquer Kit* your own

- Free meditations, contracts, a budget worksheet, and other bonuses from me that you can download at shetakesontheworld.com/conquerkitbonuses

This is going to be so, so fun! I can't wait to see what you create, and I hope you'll share your progress with me on social media **@nataliemacneil**. Let's dive in.

1

Get in the Flow

mantra

I am exactly where I need to be.

— @NATALIEMACNEIL #CONQUERKIT

STEP 1: GET IN THE FLOW

Before we dive in, I want you to take a minute to honor where you are right now.

It takes loads of courage to actually follow through on building a business. Do you ever have moments when you think, "Am I really doing this?" Yes, you really are, and that's something to celebrate.

In this first step of *The Conquer Kit*, you'll get laser focused on what you really want and why you want it. Whether you're already crystal clear on your business vision or you're still figuring it out, I will guide you through a meditation that aligns you with the kind of future you want to create for yourself. You will identify who you want to serve through your business. Then you will clear out the clutter in your life that will, without a doubt, block your flow.

Flow is your natural state, or at least it should be. Being in the flow means your business brings you more joy than stress. You don't feel totally drained after meeting with a particular client or working on a project. Flow means you're excited to get up and work on your business because your work lights you up, and you get a rush from sharing that light with others too.

Take a deep breath, and get ready to be in your flow zone.

MAY WHAT I DO FLOW FROM ME LIKE A RIVER, NO FORCING
AND NO HOLDING BACK, THE WAY IT IS WITH CHILDREN.
— RAINER MARIA RILKE

Soul-Stirring Future Success Meditation

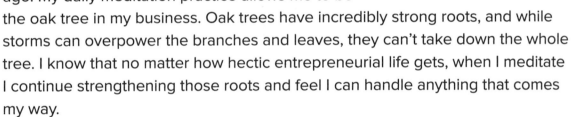

⏱ **15 MINUTES**

Meditation has been a big part of my life ever since a monk invited me to sit in stillness for a few minutes when I was traveling through Asia. That was a decade ago. My daily meditation practice allows me to be the oak tree in my business. Oak trees have incredibly strong roots, and while storms can overpower the branches and leaves, they can't take down the whole tree. I know that no matter how hectic entrepreneurial life gets, when I meditate I continue strengthening those roots and feel I can handle anything that comes my way.

For this exercise, it really doesn't matter if you have a regular meditation practice or you've never tried meditating before. For now, think of this as daydreaming.

You can listen to the guided audio version of this meditation at shetakesontheworld.com/conquerkitbonuses.

Sit or lie comfortably with your eyes closed and your palms up. Take a few core breaths, expanding your diaphragm with your inhalation and contracting it with every exhalation. Allow every part of your body to relax.

Imagine it is twelve months from now. Ask yourself, "What do I really want and where do I want to be?" Visualize where you're living, what you're working on in your business, what you're really proud of, who your biggest supporters are.

Don't put any limits on yourself right now and don't judge your dreams. If something comes to mind that you think sounds crazy, impossible, or unrealistic, honor it anyway.

Inhale potential and possibility; exhale your doubts and fears.

When you're done with the meditation, write down anything and everything that came to mind about where you want to be one year from now.

Conquer Your Clutter

⏱ **HALF DAY**

Sometimes our lives are too full for our mission, our goals, and the purpose we are meant to achieve on the planet. A crowded life does not equal a fulfilling life.

> GOALS NEED SPACE TO EXPAND.
> — @NATALIEMACNEIL #CONQUERKIT

Before you can make space for opportunities, growth, and success, you need to identify areas of your life that lack order and harmony. What are the attention grabbers that pull you away from your goals?

The key to conquering clutter is believing you can. Hold that intention with every fiber of your being, and you can make space for your dreams to come true. Count solely on your keepers—the most essential things that sustain you, the people who offer you a well-spring of support.

To get started, pick one day this week to clear out a frequently used area of your home—a desk, a bedroom closet, a kitchen utility drawer, or a cabinet. Give your day a fun name like Tackle Tuesday or Weed-Out Wednesday. You'll need markers, sticky notes, and one or more "donate" boxes. Group similar items together as you sort.

For items you're unsure about, attach a sticky note and come back to them in a week. The longer they sit unused, the more obvious it will be they need to go. If something doesn't simplify your life, consider removing it. You might sense resistance to letting go. Recognize your internal clutter for what it is and kiss it good-bye. You'll feel fantastically light after.

TO CHANGE SKINS, EVOLVE INTO NEW CYCLES, I FEEL ONE HAS TO LEARN TO DISCARD. IF ONE CHANGES INTERNALLY, ONE SHOULD NOT CONTINUE TO LIVE WITH THE SAME OBJECTS. THEY REFLECT ONE'S MIND AND THE PSYCHE OF YESTERDAY. I THROW AWAY WHAT HAS NO DYNAMIC, LIVING USE.

—ANAÏS NIN

Write about how you feel now that you've conquered your clutter:

Slay Your Dragons

⏱ **10 MINUTES**

When you know who you are, what you want, and why you really want it, is there anything that can stop you from achieving success?

Dragons.

> ALL THAT WE ARE IS THE RESULT OF WHAT WE HAVE THOUGHT.
> — BUDDHA

Of course, I'm not talking about green, scaly, overgrown lizards. I'm talking about those moments of self-doubt that we all encounter on overcast Tuesday afternoons.

I don't want to be a failure.

It's going to be so hard to get where I want to be.

I don't think I could charge higher rates because I would lose my customers.

I feel so far away from my dreams, I don't know how to get started.

Do I really need what I want?

Do any of these sound familiar to you?

Our personal dragons stand in the way of what we want most and breathe fire at us as we work toward achieving our dreams. They're also shape-shifters, taking on forms like fear, doubt, procrastination, and unworthiness. They feed on our limiting beliefs and grow more powerful, making them harder to fight if we don't keep our minds in check.

In one of the best-selling mindset and money books of all time, *Think and Grow Rich*, author Napoleon Hill makes a strong case for mindset being the key ingredient to success, no matter what you choose to do in your life. Mindset mastery is something most successful trailblazers do and it's vital for you to bring your dreams to life.

Slaying your dragons will be one of the biggest challenges of your life. Fortunately, you can get to a point where conquering your dragons is pretty easy and something you'll be able to do with a single thought. Really!

The first step to battling your dragons is naming them. Let's start by writing out any and all negative thoughts or limiting beliefs that hold you back from achieving your greatness.

Let me help you get started by sharing a few of the dragons that I battled when I first launched my business:

- I don't know where to start. Everyone else seems so far ahead of me.

- I'm totally overwhelmed by technology. I don't know the first thing about social media or blogs or coding.

- I have no idea how to deal with clients. I don't understand contracts and I'm terrible at negotiating prices. I'm worried I'll constantly be undercutting my own rates.

What dragons are you currently battling?

See It Through

Did you get all those dragons out and onto the page? Wonderful. Feels good, doesn't it? We often give these dragons less credit than they deserve. We imagine our subconscious thoughts don't carry much weight or affect our choices or our behavior. We think we can work around them with a few sticky notes and a good spreadsheet.

While those things might help, limiting beliefs can have a staggering effect on your emotional well-being, your business, and your day-to-day life. In fact, you might be amazed at how a belief you have about your business could affect your health and even your romantic relationship. But we're going to use this exercise to uncover those deeper, long-term effects so we can get rid of the underlying beliefs.

Let me give you an example to get the ball rolling.

A common limiting belief is a fear of failing. The effect of that belief might run pretty deep:

I'm worried I will fail.

How will that belief affect your business?

Well, for starters I don't take action toward my big goals because I'm afraid of failing and getting criticized for creating what I want to create.

Then what happens? How does that make you feel?

Then I feel like I'm in a stagnant place in my business because I'm not taking action towards what I really want.

And how does that make you feel?

That stagnation makes me get really frustrated. My frustration leads to further doubts about whether I'm good enough to reach my goals.

And then...

I take my frustration out on my family and friends and when they mirror my frustration I tell myself, "They just don't understand." This strains on our relationships.

Do you see how much damage one limiting belief can do?

Now it's your turn — consider those dragons and limiting beliefs. Consider how they'll affect your business and how that will make you feel.

I believe ....

And how will that affect my business?

And then what happens?

And how does that make me feel?

I believe ....

And how will that affect my business?

And then what happens?

And how does that make me feel?

I believe ....

And how will that affect my business?

And then what happens?

And how does that make me feel?

Have I convinced you? Are you ready to get rid of those dragons now that you know how they can influence other things in your life? Wonderful. The next exercise will help you do just that!

From *Limiting* to *Limitless*

⏱ **20 MINUTES**

You're capable of amazing things. You've no time for negative self-chatter or thoughts that bring you down and prevent you from meeting your goals.

Think about this: If you have a glass of crisp, fresh water and you put one drop of poison into it, you've lost that whole glass of H2O. It's the same with your mindset.

You have to protect your mind like a glass of fresh water. Before a single drop of poison can fall into your glass you have to catch it. Once caught, you can let it go. Imagine it disintegrating into bright white light. Sweet release.

Go through each of your limiting beliefs and determine the opposite of the limiting belief—this new thought is your limitless belief. I recommend you write your limitless beliefs on sticky notes and put these affirmations somewhere you'll see them often.

But before you get out the sticky notes, I want to say one important thing about creating affirmations: You have to actually believe them. If you don't quite believe the statements you're writing, change them up to something you *do* feel aligned with.

For example, if you don't believe you will succeed beyond your wildest dreams, create an affirmation like this: "I am open to the possibility of believing that I will indeed succeed beyond my wildest dreams."

LIMITING BELIEF	LIMITLESS BELIEF

Your Intention Words

⏱ **15 MINUTES**

Let's set an intention for this epic plan you're creating, and for the next twelve months of your business. I choose a different intention word or two for each fresh new year.

To get you thinking about the perfect word for you, here are some intention words from the Conquer Club community, as well as ones I've used in the past:

LIMITLESS	BALANCED	MAGNETIC
CONQUER	CLARITY	ON PURPOSE
EXPAND	PARTNERSHIP	CONTRIBUTION
FOCUSED	UNBOUNDED	LEAD
FREEDOM	HEART-DRIVEN	OPEN DOORS
ALIGNMENT	SUPPORTED	RISE

Cut and paste, draw, or write your intention word on the next page.

MY INTENTION WORDS

Your Business Beacon

⏱ **30 MINUTES**

Beacons have been used for centuries to guide people. Beacons take many forms: fires in the distance that help people find their way through the dark or lighthouses that help countless ships find the shore.

Your business beacon is your ultimate mission. Your beacon lights your path and guides you on your entrepreneurial journey.

Consider the following questions before writing your own business beacon:

- What difference do you want to make in the lives of your customers?

- What are you working on that will matter years from now?

- How are you different from your competitors?

- What do you love most about what you do?

- Big or small, how are you changing the world?

It's time to write your own business beacon. Keep in mind that there is no right or wrong way of writing your business beacon, and it's not set in stone. My business beacon continues to evolve as I grow personally and professionally. **To get you started, here's my own current business beacon:**

I WILL LIGHT UP THE WORLD BY EMPOWERING MILLIONS OF WOMEN TO REALIZE THEIR GREATEST POTENTIAL AND CONTRIBUTE THEIR GIFTS AND TALENTS THROUGH ENTREPRENEURSHIP.

I'd love to hear your intention word and business beacon. Share it with me on social media @nataliemacneil.

It's time to write your own business beacon below:

Conqueror Archetype Quiz

⏱ **20 MINUTES**

Now that you've cleared the clutter and have clarity around your intention and who you serve, it's time to discover your Conqueror Archetype.

While I can't take credit for the overall concept of archetypes (Carl Jung was the first to define them in the early twentieth century!) — I've carefully crafted Conqueror Archetypes that will help you honor and leverage your unique strengths.

Go through each question below and choose the answer that resonates with you most. Don't overthink it and feel free to select two answers if there's a tie you can't break. Ready, set, answer!

The Questions

When you're moving forward with a big new project, what's your mantra?

a. I've got this. No questions asked.

b. I've got a newer, better way to do this. Let's think outside the box!

c. Let's go bigger, better, and more beautiful. We'll figure out the details later.

d. We can make it happen. We just have to go step by step.

e. Smooth and steady rocks the launch.

f. Always have one eye on giving back.

g. Let's make it a beautiful experience. It's nothing if it's not gorgeous.

h. Let's get the right product to the right people with the right words.

When someone on your team is talking about you, how do they describe you?

a. She's a born leader.

b. She's not afraid to kick the status quo out on its butt.

c. She's a fearless creative!

d. She can make anything happen.

e. She's got a brilliant brain for the tiny details.

f. She gives, gives, and gives.

g. She can find the beauty in anything.

h. She's an authentic marketing maven.

If your business grows to a level that gives you significant wealth, what are you most likely to spend your money on?

a. A luxurious life with designer clothes, exotic vacations, and a sexy car

b. Kickstarter campaigns, and funding new dreams

c. Art pieces and stunning interior design

d. New systems and team members to scale your business, beautifully

e. High-end electronics and gadgets

f. Starting a global nonprofit or foundation

g. Your own art studio and supplies

h. Conferences and business-oriented retreats

It's Sunday afternoon. Where are we most likely to find you?

a. Having brunch with your girlfriends at the latest swanky hotspot

b. Teaching others a whole new way to do XYZ

c. Journaling or painting

d. Gardening in your backyard, or working on a home improvement project

e. Creating a couple of extra tutorial videos for your staff

f. Volunteering at a local shelter

g. Soaking in entertainment – movies, plays, art galleries, and poetry readings

h. Working on a manuscript

In your perfect world, the products you create would...

a. Rake in a wonderful profit

b. Challenge the status quo and change the way people look at things

c. Inspire others to be their best selves

d. Run almost completely independently, so you can move on to other things

e. Meet all goals and deadlines without a hitch

f. Make a global impact, and transform the planet for the better

g. Invoke a new appreciation of beauty and style

h. Become the product everyone's talking about (in the best way!)

Pick a purpose word that most resonates with you:

a. Leader

b. Trailblazer

c. Groundbreaker

d. Maker

e. Facilitator

f. Liberator

g. Catalyst

h. Ambassador

Let's time travel! Which word describes you best as a kid?

a. The Boss

b. A Rebel

c. Imaginative

d. Earnest

e. Helpful

f. Generous

g. Determined

h. A Chatterbox

Which one of these songs could be your anthem?

a. "Run the World (Girls)" – Beyoncé

b. "Revolution" – The Beatles

c. "Daydream" – Lupe Fiasco featuring Jill Scott

d. "Let's Get It Started" – The Black Eyed Peas

e. "Roar" – Katy Perry

f. "Heal the World" – Michael Jackson

g. "Try" – Colbie Caillat

h. "Your Song" – Elton John

If you're part of a larger project, which role would you rather have?

a. The boss lady! I love to run the ship.

b. The pioneer! I adore uncovering new ways to do things.

c. Visionary! I can visualize the whole thing, start to finish.

d. Concept architect! I'm a whiz at giving form and shape to the larger vision.

e. Behind-the-scenes superhero! I pride myself in designing a back end that runs beautifully.

f. Fierce philanthropist! Giving back to the globe is my heart's work.

g. Idea-centric innovator! Let's make a thing of beauty together.

h. Hype girl! Getting the word out about great projects is my jam.

Finish this sentence: I can't live without...

a. My team (present and future!); they're the wind beneath my wings

b. Pioneering ideas and the platforms where they can take root

c. My journal and vision board

d. My mastermind partners and brilliant collaborators

e. My interactive, color-coded, hyper-organized calendar

f. My volunteer activities

g. Art, music, dance, books, and movies

h. My social media peeps and all-time favorite publications

The Archetypes

Tally up how many answers you had for each letter. Put a big #1 next to your most popular letter. Put a #2 next to your second most popular letter. These are your primary and secondary archetypes. You'll find the full descriptions on the next four pages.

a =

b =

c =

d =

e =

f =

g =

h =

Mostly a's: The Queen

She was born to be a fearless leader. The Queen has no trouble seeing her goals to completion and taking responsibility for her actions whether she succeeds or fails. She's also a natural when it comes to directing large groups, helping everyone feel connected and appreciated for contributing to the effort as a whole. Because she is always pouring energy into her passions, her peers look up to her, and she rises to the top of almost every community she enters.

HER CHALLENGE: Because she's a natural leader and used to commanding respect, the Queen can sometimes seem arrogant. She needs to be careful not to slip into an egocentric mindset.

Mostly b's: The Revolutionary

She walks to the beat of her own drum and has a clear vision of how she's going to smash the status quo. She's almost never satisfied with the expected and walks a path that's in defiance of "business as usual." She appreciates originality in all its forms — and expresses it in every way she can, from her art to her wardrobe to how she spends her time.

HER CHALLENGE: Because of the Revolutionary's dislike of the expected, she can sometimes get lost trying to replace tried and true processes with her own approach. Not all rules can be broken without consequences and the Revolutionary needs to be prepared to take responsibility for all actions no matter how a situation turns out.

Mostly c's: The Dreamer

This masterful big-picture thinker can visualize how new ideas, products, and services can make an impact on people's lives. She's a visionary and strong-minded creative, and she has a knack for doing things in a way that stands out as distinctly "her." This sets her apart (seemingly effortlessly) from her would-be competitors. Ultimately, the Dreamer is here to change the world in ways both big and small.

HER CHALLENGE: She's a visionary but a daydreamer, too. She's never short on ideas but can have trouble with the follow-through. She sometimes struggles to create tools and systems that would allow her to breathe life into her concepts and big plans.

Mostly d's: The Builder

She's fantastic at giving form and shape to any concept presented to her, with just an outline or blueprint to go by. The builder is gifted at putting other people's conceptual pieces together with ease and adding to them to create results even stronger than the original vision. She's a methodical team player and will work step by step on small sections until the full concept is brought to life.

HER CHALLENGE: She can get frustrated and lost if the concept she's presented isn't completely clear. She can also get so honed in on the small pieces of the project, she won't step back to look at her work until it's finished.

Mostly e's: The Commander

She's the left-brain whiz you want behind any operation. Administrative-centric and shamelessly detail oriented, she makes an excellent team leader or business manager. She's not afraid to streamline even the tiniest element of a project and can manage any enterprise with deftness and skill.

HER CHALLENGE: She can be a micromanager and tends to have a very rigid sense of how things must be done. Flexibility or the unknown can make her nervous.

Mostly f's: The Contributor

She's a big giver and usually a philanthropist. Her big goal isn't profit, but rather the changes she can create the world. She's determined to spread good or positivity and make a serious impact. She knows she has a role to play in the future of the planet and she's going to play it. She feels the need to contribute all areas of her life — her community, family, all of her clients and customers, etc.

HER CHALLENGE: If she doesn't feel like she's making a real impact, she'll get discouraged quickly and her goals can feel meaningless. She can also struggle to approach her work from a for-profit perspective that can also do great things for the planet. She tends to put too much pressure on herself to feel that everything she does matters.

Mostly g's: The Creator

She's the *artiste* and a pure, unconventional thinker from head to toe. She has a gift for thinking outside the box and crafting things of beauty from thin air. She loves pouring all her time and energy into her process and will think of little else while she's in her zone.

HER CHALLENGE: She usually wants to stay focused on creation, so sometimes neglects the more "left brain" parts of her work and business, such as tools, administrative stuff, etc.

Mostly h's: The Messenger

She loves to teach and spread ideas — even if they aren't hers. Messengers are usually great marketers and are phenomenal at articulating a brand's overall concepts in a way that makes perfect sense to their audience. She's got great instincts for delivering materials in exciting, engaging ways and is a five-star communicator.

HER CHALLENGE: She can sometimes be so caught up in the messaging that the true meaning of what they're trying to convey gets lost in translation.

We've completed only step one and you're already making big things happen. Now, let's keep the energy up and march on to creating products people love.

2

STEP 2

Create Fantastic Things for the World (aka Your Products)

I'd never worked in fashion or retail. I just needed an undergarment that didn't exist

— SARA BLAKELY

STEP 2: CREATE FANTASTIC THINGS FOR THE WORLD (AKA YOUR PRODUCTS)

"I'd never worked in fashion or retail. I just needed an undergarment that didn't exist," said Spanx founder Sara Blakely, who built a billion-dollar empire from $5,000 in personal savings.

THIS IS IT! THE CRUX OF YOUR BUSINESS: THE GORGEOUS, CLEVER, WELL-CRAFTED PRODUCT YOU TUCK INTO THE HANDS AND HEARTS OF YOUR CUSTOMERS.

I bet you're brimming with amazing product ideas for your business, so we'll look at different sets of products and how to create a product funnel. We'll talk about the people you serve, and what needs and wants your products fulfill. We will tap into our entrepreneurial DNA and generate new ideas, and make decisions about which of our brightest ideas deserve our undivided attention and tender loving care right now.

If you are already clear on your current and future products, you can still use the following exercises to make sure your product offerings are in total alignment with your vision, values, and the needs of your customers. If you feel 100 percent aligned with what you're offering the world, it's perfectly OK to skip some of the exercises.

Beautiful Product Brainstorm

⏱ 3 HOURS

You'll need

- A camera (the camera on your phone will do)

- A small notebook

- Comfortable walking shoes

- Your own fabulous taste ;)

This mission is designed to get you up 'n' out of this book, really thinking about the kind of products and customer experiences you love and why. It will give you a ton of inspiration fuel, so you can start dreaming up ways to craft similar experiences for your buyers.

Sometime in the next week, head out to some of your favorite retail stores or restaurants—the ones you walk into and think "I wish my house looked like this!"

While you're in there (be sure to visit at least three different locations), take a good look around you at the products, decor, or small customer-centric details that catch your eye. Gorgeous packaging, charming notes or sayings on the walls, and so on.

After that, take yourself on a date to your favorite café or restaurant for a little treat and at least half an hour of inspired, inspiration-fueled brainstorming.

Review your pictures and record your observations on the left side of the table below.

What did you like and why? What did you keep coming back to? Then, on the right side, jot down some ideas about how you can create similar beautiful customer experiences in your own business and products.

OBSERVATIONS	HOW CAN I CREATE SIMILAR EXPERIENCES?

The Things You *Want* to Be Doing

⏱ **20 MINUTES**

You're an incredibly smart and talented human (obviously; you bought this book!) and there are any number of things you *could* do to make money. Give yourself over to fantasy, remove pesky obstacles like time and expense, and write down all the products/services/offerings you could, theoretically, do.

Don't censor or limit yourself or even confine yourself to one career field. Maybe you're a marketing expert who also happens to love dogs and the green expanses of the outdoors—it's totally OK to write down both "dog walking service" and "one-day marketing intensive for brick-and-mortar businesses." Also write down your skills that you're not that pumped about. If you used to do bookkeeping (and still know how), add it to the list.

Things I *Could* Do ...

Now it's time to narrow the field a bit by thinking about what you actually like doing. Maybe you understand how to balance the books, but you have no interest in ever doing that again.

Things I *Want* to Do ...

And finally, it's time to get realistic. When you consider things like available time, learning curves, geographic location, and work ethic, what are the things you can do?

Things I *Can* Do ...

The People You Serve

⏱ 1 HOUR

Your business will impact people's lives far beyond your own.

People will read what you write and change their minds. They might use your products to feel happier and more connected to their lives and the world around them.

But before you can change lives and open hearts, you need to know *whose* lives you're changing, *which* hearts you're opening. Busy moms? Mid-level managers who've become jaded in their careers? Young women struggling with their romantic relationships? Empty nesters ready for adventure? We're going to start with the basics—who you're helping and the lives they're currently leading.

I like to imagine my clients as characters in a story; I picture every aspect of their lives—down to name, age, location, *and* coffee preference. I want to know what lights them up and what makes them tick.

Gina is funny and outgoing. She lives in a loft on the north side of Chicago with her boyfriend and much-loved, poorly trained rescue dog. She works as a personal trainer at a high-

end gym, but she's losing faith in the fitness industry. She's thinking of changing careers, but she's not sure what she wants to do or where to start. She's inspired by setting and achieving physical goals (she's run three triathlons this year), but she struggles with psychological or professional goals. She needs structure and training schedules to make things happen. She's pretty happy with her life, but she's haunted by a certain feeling of "Is this it?" She spends her weekends hiking, cooking, and drinking a lot of black coffee.

There are two reasons we create these client stories:

1. It's fun!

2. We're describing our ideal clients and once we know our ideal clients, we're better able to build a business that will attract them.

Create an insanely detailed picture of your ideal client.

Is your dream client a man or a woman? What's her name?

How old is she?

Where does she live? Which city? Which state?

Is she outdoorsy or more metropolitan?

Does she live in the suburbs? The city center? What's her home like?

What's her job? How much does she earn?

What's her relationship status? Does she have children? Pets?

How does she spend her free time?

What TV shows does she watch? What does she read—
which websites, books, magazines?

What kind of outfit would you usually see her wearing?

What problems does she wish she could solve?

What does she eat for breakfast?

What's her most used smartphone app?

What is she willing to splurge on?

How would her best friend describe her if that
friend were being totally honest?

What's one *big* dream she's open about?

What's one *big* dream she's more private about?

Whew! Feels like you know her intimately, doesn't it? On the next page, write a
paragraph about your dream client's average Wednesday. Give her — or him —
a name, and paste in an image from a magazine that helps you better visualize
this person.

Come back to this exercise whenever you need a fresh jolt of inspiration to create incredible services and products your people will l-o-v-e (and buy again and again).

MY IDEAL CLIENT

Assess Their Struggles

⏱ 1 TO 2 HOURS

It's time to home in on your customers' struggles so you can create the best products and services that will address those struggles and solve those problems. Remember the stories you wrote about your customers in the last exercise?

Now it's time to zoom in on:

a. What your dream customers are struggling with

b. How you can help them

And how are you going to do that? By doing your research, or just straight-up asking them.

ONLINE: Start easy. Do a Google search for forums or online communities frequented by your potential clients. Do you want to work with stay-at-home moms? Cyclists? Independent musicians? Simply search for "message board [potential clients]" and then give yourself over to some good old-fashioned sleuthing.

Here are a few questions to get you started:

- What are they complaining about?

- What solutions are they suggesting to each other?

- What platforms and products do they mention?

- Do they have complaints about those products or platforms? If so, what are they?

- Can this problem be solved with a one-size-fits-all solution? Or do they need customized help?

- How would their lives be improved if you could solve this problem for them?

- Does this problem cross age/cultural/geographic lines within this community? Or is it limited to one subset within the group? (For example, stay-at-home moms who live in urban areas or cyclists who commute to work on city streets.)

- How much do you think these people would pay to have this problem solved?

Struggle Assessment in Real Life

⏱ 3 TO 5 HOURS OVER THE COURSE OF A FEW WEEKS

Now that we've described our ideal client down to her shoes and pets, we're going to investigate the real-life versions. Like, the real, live human versions.

Let's say your ideal client is a thirty- to forty-five-year-old woman. She's a wife and mom; is active; and has a busy, successful career. You suspect this type of woman would benefit from a meal delivery service, but you'd like to pick some brains before you launch something big.

How do you find people to interview? Through social media and the friends you already have. You should aim for five to eight interviews.

Here's a list to get you started:

EMAIL: If you know a few people who meet the criteria of your ideal client, email them (individually!) and ask if they'd be willing to chat with you for twenty minutes or allow you to buy them dinner, in exchange for answering some questions. If you're not buying them dinner, always offer them something as a thank you—a gift card for Amazon or Starbucks, for example.

If you need more interviews, ask them if they know anyone who meets your criteria.

FACEBOOK: Write an update telling your friends that you're seeking insight from people who are [insert your criteria here]. Again, tell them that you'd be happy to buy them dinner in exchange for their time or to send them a gift card. Here's a Facebook template to get you started:

Hi friends! I'm working on a new project that I'm pretty excited about—but I need your help! I need insight from a few [insert criteria here]. Is that you? If it is—and you're here in [name of your city]—I'd love to buy you dinner while I pick your brain. If you're not nearby, I'd be more than happy to kick you an Amazon gift card as a thank-you. If you're keen, drop me a line at [email address] and we can get started! The whole thing takes less than 20 minutes so it's pretty painless!

YOUR PROFESSIONAL NETWORKS: Are you part of any associations? Networking groups? Alumni groups? I bet you are and I bet those groups are rife with people who could help you. Write up a slightly more professional version of the Facebook template and share it with your groups.

Here is a chart to help you stay organized:

PLATFORM I USE TO FIND PEOPLE	DATE	NUMBER OF RESPONSES	CONTACT INFO FOR INTERVIEWEES

Ask the Big Questions

So you've found some of those elusive ideal clients in real life. They've accepted your invitation to brain-picking. Now what do you ask them?

Don't overthink this, dear Conqueror. The purpose of these interviews is to understand your ideal client a bit better. What are her struggles? How much would she be willing to pay for your services or products?

When you're interviewing these people, begin the conversation with a thirty-second explanation of your product. Tell them that they're in your target demographic, which is why you want their input!

Here are a few questions to get you started:

- What was your knee-jerk reaction when I told you about this product? Be honest!

- Do you feel like it solves a problem that you're struggling with?

- If it doesn't solve the problem, what would solve the problem?

- Have you tried to solve this problem before? If so—did that solution work? If not—why not?

- What would you be willing to pay for this product or service?

- How would you want to receive this product or service? (One on one? In the mail? In a store? As part of a group?)

- Do you have any suggestions for how I could make this better/more appealing/more helpful?

Release, Review, and Refine

⏱ **45 MINUTES**

OK, Conqueror—since we've been talking about all these products and services you could be offering, it's time to put all your great ideas in one place—and I mean *all of them.*

So go grab your notebooks and journals. Hunt down those scraps of ideas you jotted on napkins and sticky notes. The one- or two-liners saved in the notes app on your phone. The blurbs in emails or blog posts that made you say, "Wait a second . . . maybe I can use that!"

Then, once they're all together, I'll help you zero in on exactly what you want to focus on.

Ready? Here we go.

PART 1: Release

Write down every single product idea you've got in the space below. Put it all in there. Yep, even the stuff that's just been floating around in your head. Seeing all of it in one place will help you get clear about what you want to focus on and which concepts you feel most excited about.

PART 2: Review

Considering what you know now, take a look at the ideas you've jotted down and see what jumps out at you. What options would be the best fit for your audience, their needs, and the way you want to work?

PART 3: Refine

Circle one to three ideas you feel would be the best fit for your audience and direction. (Do *not* go over the three idea limit!) In a perfect world, you'd circle only one concept to invest your energy into, but you can choose three if the ideas build on each other. This will help you focus your efforts on these specific concepts, so you can really pour yourself into your ideas.

Remember: No matter how good you are, you can't do everything at once.

Trust me, I've tried. (And because you're reading this book, I know you probably have too!)

Narrowing down your selection forces you to get really clear on what you want to work on, and why.

A, B, C Product Plan

⏱ **1½ HOURS**

When you're planning and plotting your products, keep future products and spin-offs in mind, too. Make use of all that brainstorming!

This very book is inspired by my first book *She Takes on the World* and by my Conquer Club group. You see how I did that? Built one product on top of the others? When you create the right products, they build on themselves and support sales of each other. It's obvious to your customers that if they liked Product A, they'll loooove Product B, and they should definitely keep their eyes open for Product C.

Let's start with an example! Let's say you're a travel blogger and fledgling travel agent. Here are the products you might create:

PRODUCT A: Free, 10-page ebook about how to pack for a month in your carry-on

This ebook also includes links to all your social media profiles, links to helpful blog posts, and a discount code for Product B. People must give their email address in order to get this freebie, and having that email address will allow you to follow up with valuable content and future offers.

PRODUCT B: $75 self-paced ecourse about solo travel

This is an eighteen-thousand-word ebook that helps readers travel alone confidently. It includes an audio version, tons of worksheets, one group call, links to your social media profiles, and a discount code for your trip-planning services.

PRODUCT C: $400 trip-planning consult

This is a one-week process in which you start with a phone call to your client about her trip and her expectations for the trip. You assemble a list of interesting and unique lodging, dining, and outing options for her. Once she's approved these options, you make the reservations for her.

See how cleverly these products feed into each other? Let's get you started on your own set of products! When you're designing your products, it's best to start in the middle and work outward—meaning we'll start with your mid-level B products, which are frequently the most popular.

PRODUCT B QUESTIONS

- Based on your research, what problems do your ideal clients face?

- How can you make your product better/different/more successful than other products that address the same issue?

- When you take into account your feelings about the different types of products, would you like to create a physical product, a consulting offering, or an info product?

- Based on what you'd like to earn and what your ideal clients want to pay, what's the right price for this?

- How will you promote Product C with this product?

PRODUCT A QUESTIONS

- What free sample can you create that relates to your Product B?

- What form do you want this freebie to take? An ebook? A series of videos? A physical sample?

- What action do you want people to take in order to get this freebie? Sign up for your email list? Follow you on Facebook? Share your article?

- How will you promote your other products with Product A?

PRODUCT C QUESTIONS

- If this is your highest priced offering, how will you customize it to make it feel like a good value for this price tag?

- Based on the success of Product B and the information you have about your ideal clients, what's the right price for this?

- How much time do you expect to spend on each Product C? How many of these can you do/sell/make each month?

Your Product Creation Checklist

🕑 1½ HOURS

When you're gearing up to create and release a product, it's important that you have crystal-like clarity about your audience. Understanding the ins and outs of your product, who it's for, the solution it provides, and so forth—these are all essential for avoiding any potential obstacles and streamlining your production path.

So, before you jump into the "build it" phase of your product, run through the following questions:

Is there a demand for this product? Why?

You can have a quality product, but no demand equals no income.

In contrast, when you create a product people really need, your sales process will be much easier and you'll know you're truly helping people with your offerings.

If you're not 100 percent certain about the potential demand, survey your audience, and use the Google AdWords Keyword Planner app to check the monthly search volume for keywords related to your product.

What's your sales strategy exactly?

Selling a one-time information product might not make you a huge profit on its own, but selling off the back of your other product has huge moneymaking potential.

Choose an info product that's suitable for follow-up products and updates that you can offer to your existing customers at a discount. If the original product is good quality and really helps your customers, they are likely to buy the follow-up product.

How will you make this look, sound, and feel professional? If you can't do it yourself, who will you hire to help you?

Presentation is just as important as content when establishing the credibility of your product (if not a little more so). A great logo, clear graphics, and a professional, high-impact design will help increase your sales and gain the loyalty of your customers.

Does this product follow legal requirements?

I highly recommend seeking advice from a lawyer when creating products, so consider booking an appointment with one!

Double- and triple-check that you're not breaking any copyright or trademark laws with your products (this includes using copyrighted images, fonts, etc.). Also, if you're including personal views and opinions, add a disclaimer that states you're not providing professional advice.

Disclaimers are 100 percent necessary when giving advice on health and nutrition, so don't release a product without them. If someone follows your advice, and something goes wrong, such a statement will protect you.

Are you using enough images? Where and what kind?

A few well-chosen pictures can really lift your product and make it look more professional. Photographs are available from lots of image sites on the web at an affordable price. In the provided space, cut and paste images that showcase your product as well as the benefits, features, and happiness it will bring to your customers.

Will you include templates, checklists, and questionnaires? What will you be using?

People love questionnaires and checking off boxes.

Wherever possible, include one or more of these tools in your product. They allow clients to check their progress and provide a summary of important data.

Do you plan to include a resource list? Who's going to be on it?

Adding a list of resources within your product can add massive value. Your list can include organizations, websites, and other online resources that might be useful to your customers.

(This can also be a moneymaker for you if you're an affiliate for any of the resources you include. Feel free to use your affiliate link, but always disclose when you do!)

Do you have a system in place to collect case studies and testimonials? What is it?

Always ask people for testimonials and personal experiences with your product. This stuff is sales page gold.

Proof that other clients have benefited from your services builds trust and shows that you're a professional. A customer who endorses your product or service is worth so, so much more than paid advertising.

Are you offering a money-back guarantee?
Why or why not?

If you believe that what you're offering will provide the value you promise, then you have no reason to withhold a money-back guarantee. You know it's going to work, so where's the risk?

Trust that people will not abuse this guarantee, because few do.

Are you putting your best foot forward?
How do you know?

This sounds obvious but make sure what you've created is something you're super proud of. Your product is a reflection of your business, your brand, and you. If you're not sure, ask a few beta testers for their unbiased opinion.

Break It Down—Even Further

⏱ 30 MINUTES

One of the most common complaints that I hear about products or services is that they're overwhelming, have too many features, are too advanced. Surprising, right?

Many of us get caught up in delivering The.Best.Product.Ever., incorporating every piece of knowledge we have and overwhelming our customers. We think we're giving them amazing value for their money; they think they're drowning in a flood of information.

Think about your dream customer, her needs, and how you can simplify your solutions. I bet your customers would prefer a twenty-page ebook about mastering Twitter over a two-hundred-page treatise about mastering every single social media platform. I bet they'd also prefer a cookbook with twenty recipes, each of which has five ingredients, over a two-hundred-page tome filled with fifteen-ingredient dishes.

Another benefit to breaking down your offerings into simpler, easier pieces? You're not giving away all your expertise in one or two offerings and since your offerings are smaller, you'll be able to price them more affordably and more people will be able to buy them.

Product/Offering A: _____

How can I make this easier, simpler, more digestible?

Product/Offering B: _____

How can I make this easier, simpler, more digestible?

Product/Offering C: _____

How can I make this easier, simpler, more digestible?

Pinpoint Your Price

⏱ **1 HOUR**

Despite what you may have heard, pricing your products properly isn't actually a science. It's an art.

One of the most essential things to keep in mind when coming up with prices and setting goals for your products or services in the future is this: Branding really is everything.

When you're looking at products from two different companies, the same offerings might have drastically different prices. For example, you might buy a $10 shirt from H&M that looks quite a bit like a $1,000 shirt from Dolce & Gabbana. They're both cotton, they're both drapey, they're both a flattering shade of blue. But one costs a hundred times as much.

In the case of the overpriced shirt, we see that perceived value is what is the most important. While the raw product costs may be similar, people will buy the D&G shirt for the name alone. Luxury brands create value with their name and perception.

With services-based businesses, you have to look at the value you're providing to your clients. It's vital that you place a clear-cut value on what you do for people and the changes and improvements that will occur after they become your clients.

If you are selling a physical product, you need to first consider the price of your materials or the wholesale price you paid for the product. This is your *cost of goods*, and we'll dive deeper into how this fits into your overall financial picture a little bit later in the book. Your markup on the cost of goods needs to cover all your expenses and the cost of your time so you can earn a great salary.

I find valuing your own time is one of the trickiest aspects of pricing for many entrepreneurs. If you offer a service like management consulting or life coaching, the major cost to the business will be your time. You don't need to buy machinery or wholesale products, but you do need to consider the hours you spend on education and development. If you are selling products, you'll need to consider the cost of your time as well. Think about the time you spend promoting your business, talking to customers, networking, and all the other hats you wear as an entrepreneur.

Let's get clarity on your pricing:

A. How much do you want to earn over the next twelve months?

B. To meet that goal, how much do you need to earn each month?

To calculate how much you'll need to earn, you'll need to consider:

1. The expenses you must be able to cover from your income like rent, office supplies, professional advice, travel, phone, and Internet connection

2. The dreams you want to fulfill in the coming year (and how much they cost)

3. Business expenses you need to cover

4. Your ideal take-home pay (your answer to question A)

   Add all of these together, and that's how much revenue you'll need to bring in!

   Here's an example:

EXPENSES AND DREAMS		AMOUNT
Expenses	Office rent	$2,400 per year
	Office supplies	$400 per year
	Work travel	$3,000 per year
	Virtual assistant	$3,000 per year
	Internet	$400 per year
	Phone	$1,200 per year
Dreams	3-week Mexican vacation	$5,000
Ideal take-home pay		$75,000 per year
Total		**$ 90,400 per year**

Now think about how many days a week you'd like to work. Don't forget public holidays and the three weeks in Mexico. Write the number below.

I want to work _____ days per year.

Now decide how many hours per day you'd like to work. Don't forget to deduct evenings out, taking your kids to school, doing pro-bono work, going to the gym, fitting in that painting class, and the other things you want to do that bring you happiness and align with your personal definition of success.

I want to work _____ hours per day.

Now, do the calculation:

Desired income & expenses ÷ (Days per year × Hours per day) = _____

For example, let's imagine you need to bring in $200,000 per year to cover all your business expenses and earn your desired income. You want to work two hundred days a year and five hours per day.

This gives you $200,000 ÷ (200 × 5) = $200,000 ÷ 1,000 = $200 per hour

So $200 is your ideal hourly rate. This means every hour you work needs to generate this amount, whether you're writing proposals, doing administrative tasks, or providing your service for a high-paying client.

This exercise is meant to give you some perspective. But remember, pricing your products and services is an art. You can also look at what your competitors charge to give yourself an idea of the range your price point should fall within.

As you may know by now, I let intuition guide so many of the decisions I make, and pricing is one of those things that has to feel right for me. Based on the work we've been doing in this section, list your products and services on the next page, and the price that feels right for each:

PRODUCT	PRICE THAT FEELS GOOD

3

Form the Four Pillars of Success

Start where you are.
Use what you have.
Do what you can.

— ARTHUR ASHE

STEP 3: FORM THE FOUR PILLARS OF SUCCESS

I need you to make me a promise, Conqueror. Repeat after me, please:

Even if this step doesn't feel as exciting as some of the other steps in the book and even if it starts to feel overwhelming, I'm going to stick with Natalie and work through it.

There are four nonnegotiable pillars that hold up any successful business. While they might not seem terribly fun to create, they're extremely important:

In this section we're covering the essentials that build a foundation for your business that's strong enough to support the biggest, most thrilling, most audacious dreams: yours.

You won't find too many exercises in this section, but what you *will* find is a series of mega-detailed (and easy-to-understand) to-do lists. Navigating these important-if-slightly-dry aspects of your business needn't feel overwhelming. In fact, it's totally doable. Promise!

If you dive in without these critical pieces of the puzzle, you risk creating an unwieldy business that doesn't scale as you grow. If you grow too quickly, it can feel like your work is a burden, not a pleasure. Growing a business *should* feel expansive and exciting!

Take it from me: It's *much* easier to set up and maintain great systems while your business is still small. Otherwise, you risk massive mistakes as you grow—mistakes that can leave you feeling unprepared and vulnerable.

Over the next few months, I encourage you to set aside time to work on each of the pieces and action items of Step 3. You don't have to do them all at once! Schedule a block of time each week to take care of these specific business essentials, so you can start building on your unshakeable foundation.

PILLAR 1: The Right Name

A good name is memorable, interesting, and—most important—obvious. People frequently get hung up on clever, rhyming names or something that's alliterative. If it's not immediately obvious to your customers what you're selling and what you can do for them, choose a different name.

If you're already head over heels in love with your business name and your customers love it too, you can use this pillar to name your products and services or you can just put a big checkmark on this pillar and skip over it.

Admittedly, you can't just do a few naming exercises and expect to come up with the perfect name for your business. A great name can't be forced. Sometimes you need to be patient and wait until you have that "*This is it!*" gut feeling. I've had that strong intuitive hit with my business name and product names.

The name of my blog, "She Takes on the World," actually came to me in a dream. I loved the name so much that I opened my eyes to jot down a few notes on my phone so I wouldn't forget it. The next morning, when I read over those notes, I had that full-body "*Yes, this is it!*" feeling. The rest is history, and today She Takes on the World Inc. is my own little empire.

If you're having trouble coming up with a business name that feels right, you may be able to use your own name to get started. You can launch different products, services, and packages that have unique names while staying under the umbrella of your personal name.

In many jurisdictions, using your own name allows you to act as a sole proprietor for the business without having to file formal business registration or name registration paperwork. This can help get you up and running faster, and it allows you to explore different offerings in your business. You can always choose to register another name later. This approach works better for some people—and some industries—than others. If you're opening a store, you probably want to come up with a name for the store rather than using your own name. If you're running an agency and the business isn't based on your work alone, consider a name for the business.

No matter what you decide, don't rush it. I can't stress enough how important this decision is! I've seen too many entrepreneurs change the name of their business, sometimes multiple times, because they ran with a name that didn't fully resonate.

Names That Resonate

⏱ 1 WEEK

For the next week, make a conscious effort to tune into company names that delight you. Don't over-analyze why you like them, what they mean, and how they appeal to a broader market. Simply keep an ongoing list of names that tickle your fancy.

For example, I've always loved the name of frozen yogurt company Pinkberry. The first time I saw a Pinkberry store, I immediately thought, "This is going to be fun!" I love Evernote, too—it's easy to remember and I immediately knew it was going to help me with note taking. What names appeal to you? Why? You may start to notice a pattern. I noticed I also like business names that merge two words or memorable phrases, like the book title *I Was Told There'd Be Cake*.

Naming Matrix

⏱ 1 HOUR

Grab a thesaurus for this exercise. In each of the areas within the matrix, make a list of nouns, adjectives, and verbs that resonate with you. Use the thesaurus to come up with alternate words and write those as well. Make a list of words that describe your business, too. Once you've created these separate lists, try pairing different combinations of words from each list to form names you like. Write these potential names in the middle square on the next page.

For example, let's say you're a jewelry business, and you have "bright" on your list of adjectives, "heart" on your noun list, and "jewels" on your list of words that describe your business. You could combine these to get Brightheart Jewels Company.

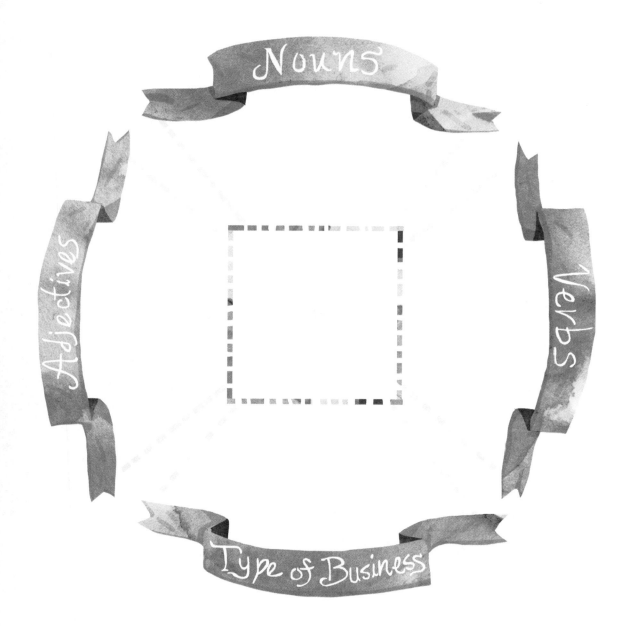

The Name Test

⏱ 10 MINUTES

For this exercise, we'll be diving into the full 360 view of the business name you've chosen, and whether it's the best fit for your growing empire.

Let's put your name to the test.

Is the name easy for people to pronounce?

Yes   No

Is the name easy for people to spell correctly?

Yes   No

Is there a URL available for it?

Yes   No

Will people be able to successfully get to the URL without you having to spell out the name for them?

Yes   No

Is your name short and sweet or a memorable phrase? For example, though She Takes on the World is a pretty long name, it's a memorable phrase.

Yes   No

Does your name contain a word that is specific to one product, limiting your options for growing the product line? For example, one of my clients was using the word *stationery* in her business name, and when she wanted to start selling planners, journals, and other products in her store she had to undergo a name change and rebranding.

Yes   No

Is there a meaning that will resonate with your audience?

Yes   No

After you finish answering all the questions, tally up the results. If there are more than two no answers, I recommend revising your business name.

When considering spelling and pronunciation, you might want to survey people you know to make sure they agree with you. One person's theatre is another person's theater! In the space provided, tally up those responses and ensure the majority of people can spell and pronounce your name correctly.

Remember, good names can take time. Even if a name passes this name test, if it doesn't feel quite right, keep tweaking. You hope to be living with this name for a long time and having to change the name down the road can be expensive.

PILLAR 2: The Right Legal Structure

When you're a good-natured, heart-centered entrepreneur, it's easy to let the legal bits slide. We want to believe that everyone is trustworthy and well intentioned, and legalese is overwhelming and confusing. But if you want to build a solid legal foundation for your business, I'd encourage you to take this mantra to heart:

Everyone signs something.

That's the golden rule attorney Kyle Durand uses when it comes to the legal foundation of my business and any business for that matter. If you want to protect your work, your profits, your kids' college fund, and your retirement funds, you must be smart about how you safeguard your business.

I also realize contracts can be totally overwhelming and all that red tape can deter people from ever building a successful business. So with the help of Kyle Durand, one of my fantastic lawyers and the founder of OurDeal, I'll help you cross off your legal essentials in this section. I'll also empower you with basic fill-in-the-blank contracts to define and clarify the relationships and expectations you have with your clients and your employees or contractors.

The exercises here will help you lay a foundation, but I strongly recommend seeking legal advice when you're starting and growing a business. I'm *not* a lawyer (surprise!) and this information is not a substitute for legal advice.

To get you started, here are some legal essentials to familiarize yourself with:

- Get a good lawyer, no matter how small your business is now. It's great to have that kind of support in your back pocket. You need an expert in your corner should you ever be surprised with a serious problem.

- Sign up for a service like OurDeal or Adobe Document Cloud eSign to make sending and electronically signing contracts a breeze for you and the people you're working with.

- Review the business entities in your country and choose the one that suits your business best. This is a very important step, but each country is different so make sure you do your research!

- Nolo it! Nolo is the largest online legal resource, and while it's not a replacement for a lawyer, it's definitely a site to bookmark and visit when you need legal information.

- Use the trademark symbol (™) on things you consider to be your intellectual property. This will give you a basic level of legal protection. For example, if someone tries to register a trademark, and you can prove you've been using it for longer, you can lay claim to that mark.

- If a trademark is critical to your business, it's good to register it. The registered trademark symbol (®) is reserved for trademarks that have indeed been registered. Not every business owner needs to register trademarks, especially if you don't have the resources to follow up with people, send cease and desist letters, and monitor the web and publications for trademark violations.

- Consult with a lawyer about the structure of your company and how it's registered. For the majority of small businesses, if you operate on a freelance or contractor basis, it's likely that you work as a sole proprietor. But, if your revenue is getting close to six figures or more, or there's a lot of personal risk you take on in your line of work, I encourage you to speak to a lawyer about whether registering as a limited liability company (LLC) or corporation would be better for tax savings, added protection, and other potential benefits.

- Depending on your area of jurisdiction, your industry, whether you have a brick-and-mortar business versus an online business, different licenses come into play. You might be surprised what businesses and offerings would require you to obtain some sort of license beyond just registering your business. Make sure you look into local, state/provincial, and national or federal licenses or permits that may be required for the type of business that you're running.

If you're not sure that you can afford a lawyer, I recommend looking at things this way: In the long run, having a legal genius on your side will save you a lot of money, a lot of stress, and a lot of energy you could be putting toward better things if something goes wrong. Trust me on this one.

When I found myself in my first tricky legal situation, I was fuming in my lawyer's office. He reassured me that everything was going to be fine because I had made smart decisions to protect myself and my growing business. He even offered to buy me a bottle of champagne to pop to celebrate.

"Celebrate?!" I cried.

"Yes, you know you've made it in business when you find yourself really needing a lawyer for something!"

That did put a smile on my face, and fortunately everything worked out because I'd followed the legal essentials I just outlined for you.

Make those key investments now and your future self will thank you.

Conquer Your Contracts

○ ONGOING

When you're starting out, you may think you don't need to worry about having contracts in place and having a lawyer. I mean, contracts are for when you're landing the big deals and making loads of money, right? I hate to burst your bubble, but at a bare minimum you need to have a contract signed for each client you work with and for each person or service provider that you hire to help you get your business off the ground.

If contracts have scared you up to this point, let me tell you that it's much scarier to face an issue with a client or one of your hires without a contract in place.

I once had a marketing client who I went over and above for on everything. In my effort to make her over-the-moon happy, I made the mistake of saying yes to just about every request she had, even when it felt like she was using me as an assistant outside the scope of the project. After my contract with this client ended, she came back to me about a year later trying to blame me for a pretty minor issue that she was experiencing. It was nothing to get so worked up about, but I later found out that the business was failing and I think she was just in a bad frame of mind and looking to place blame anywhere she could. She made some threats about legal action. To make a long story short, having a clear contract and a lawyer I could turn to really put my mind at ease.

> IF THE DEAL MATTERS TO YOU, CREATE A WRITTEN CONTRACT. IF THE RELATIONSHIP WITH YOUR CLIENT OR CONTRACTOR MATTERS, CREATE A WRITTEN CONTRACT. IF NEITHER OF THESE APPLY, CREATE A WRITTEN CONTRACT ANYWAY.
> — KYLE DURAND #CONQUERKIT

Kyle Durand is one of our Conquer Club mentors and one of our favorite lawyers. He's providing you with two contracts: a Client Agreement and an Independent Contract Agreement for people you might work with, like a virtual assistant or web developer. You can download these contracts and other bonuses at shetakesontheworld.com/conquerkitbonuses. These contracts are designed to be the absolute minimum to get you started, but for more detailed contracts that cover a variety of situations, definitely check out OurDeal.

PILLAR 3: The Right Support Systems

Would you rather dream up new products than write an operations manual? Prefer pitching ideas to onboarding new clients? Creating systems to support your business might not be particularly thrilling, but those systems are the backbone of your company.

I recommend implementing systems in your business from the get-go. These integral parts of your business will keep your day-to-day operations streamlined and they'll keep you from falling into that behind-the-curtain chaos so many entrepreneurs experience.

I've seen too many businesses let systems fall by the wayside. Without those essential puzzle pieces, things get terribly messy when you're ready to expand and scale. If you don't implement systems now, you'll just end up working backward to piece together processes for every bit of your business.

In this section, we'll cover basic systems you'll want behind the scenes so you stay on track, organized, and ready to grow.

Simple Systems Checklist

It may take you a while to check off all the items in the following list, so be gentle with yourself and give yourself a reasonable, sane timeline. Do give yourself a timeline though, and actually get this stuff on your calendar.

Have an operations manual ready to go: This baby is going to be the Bible of your business. Make sure you keep it current and easily accessible for yourself and your team. This document includes your brand's fonts and hex color codes, your invoice process and contract templates, even tutorials for uploading, tagging, and posting your social media updates. Your manual should house anything and everything your team would need to run your business without you. You'll be crafting your own operations manual in the next exercise. Get excited!

Goal completion date for this system:

Create a process for onboarding team members: While we'll talk about this on page 160, I want you to start thinking now about the way you want to welcome new people to your team. How available will you be to teach them? How are you going to make them feel welcome and quickly familiar with the way you do things? Being clear on this process is critical for managing the learning curve and helping new employees feel engaged and supported.

Goal completion date for this system:

Design a strategy for managing prospective clients: You should put a system in place to make sure you're regularly communicating with people who like what you do, but aren't quite ready to say yes yet. The most important part of this process is regular communication. If you go six months without contacting a prospect . . . she's not a prospect anymore, is she? Make sure you're clear on exactly what your business does to keep in touch with these "maybes" and encourage them to hire you again and again in the future.

Goal completion date for this system:

Implement a process for onboarding new clients: How are you attracting new clients and what happens after they decide to work with you? Which contracts should people be signing? How will you bill them? What are your plans for creating a beautiful customer experience? Ask yourself these questions so you can roll out the red carpet for new customers and clientele every time. (You'll be mapping out your process for this in just a few pages.)

Goal completion date for this system:

Apply technology to manage your online presence: Being visible takes some serious work! But, thanks to a few handy tools and apps, you can massively simplify your digital life. Some I find particularly useful: Hootsuite, Buffer, and TweetDeck for scheduling social media updates, PicMonkey and Canva for creating simple graphics, Toggl for time tracking, and Trello and Asana for project management. I've included a more comprehensive list at the end of the book, so be sure to take a peek!

If you don't already have a mailing list, you can create one for free via MailChimp and tuck a signup form right into your website. I use Infusionsoft, but you may not need such robust business management software just yet.

Goal completion date for this system:

Create Your Operations Manual

⏱ 2 HOURS TO START + ONGOING PROCESS

An operations manual is like your business Bible. It's a must-have for every single business, no matter how small or simple. It's the ridiculously detailed, nothing-held-back instructional guide for the way you run everything. Once created, someone should be able to use the guide to run your entire business, even if you have no desire to let someone take the helm. Having an operations manual also makes it significantly easier to train new hires and teach them the ins and outs of how you do business.

For this exercise, create a file on your computer or set up a private document on Google Drive or Box. You probably already have a lot of this information in different files so this might consist of a lot of copying and pasting to get everything into one organized document. This is a great task to pass off to an assistant, too.

Your operations manual should include all business essentials, like:

- Key documents and contract templates

- Template email responses

- Company policies

- Relevant copy (mini and full-length bios, elevator pitches, etc.)

- Your logo

- Your brand colors, along with the HTML color codes that match

- Best practices for blogging, promotion, social media—any work that your team will be doing

- How-to videos for tasks like uploading your blog posts, formatting images, adding footnotes, photo credits, blog post tags, scheduling your social media posts, and sending out your newsletters

Jing is an excellent service for creating tech tutorials. It makes it blissfully simple to capture your screen, while doing a personal voiceover. Even better, it's free.

Don't forget that your operations manual should be customized to you and your business. You can organize it in the way that makes the most sense for you and add your own personal touches. For example, if there are certain words or phrases you hate, be sure to add some side notes about them in your operations manual so your team, or future team, knows what kind of copy not to write for product descriptions or social media updates.

I'm big on color coding and keeping information as bite-size as possible. In your business, longer descriptions and highly detailed instructions may be required. For example, if your business is selling a type of supplement or food product, your operations manual might have very lengthy descriptions about handling, cleanup, and other requirements because you would have to adhere to strict regulations.

This is really an ongoing exercise and it should be updated regularly! Yes, it can be a tedious process, but I promise you'll thank me later for this one.

Client Welcome System

⏱ **2 HOURS**

At She Takes on the World Inc., we're a small (but soulful!) team, handling a community of thousands. How do we do it? We have a crisp, clear system for onboarding new clients. Our system shows them what they can expect now that they're in our tribe, how we work and communicate, and anything they need to fill out and sign.

No matter what business you're in, having a process for welcoming and supporting new clients is a fundamental necessity to help them feel cared for and totally loyal to you for the long term.

Here's a peek behind the curtain at the She Takes on the World client onboarding process:

PHASE 1: The Purchase

We make purchasing easy, and we walk clients through the steps to follow so they feel guided during the whole process. We also make sure they know how to get support if they have questions. If there's a contract or nondisclosure agreement that needs to be signed, do it immediately after the purchase to make it all official.

PHASE 2: Start the Client Nurture Sequence

The moment a new client walks through our virtual doors, we start sending her a sequence of emails that begin building a solid relationship. In the case of the

Conquer Club, this sequence is three weeks long because there are a lot of steps to take and we don't want to overwhelm people from the get-go.

This series of emails is already automated so it runs on its own like clockwork. We use Infusionsoft in our business because it helps us manage every piece of our growing business. Ontraport is an alternative. AWeber and MailChimp are great tools for email marketing if you're not ready for a whole business management system yet.

A: Lay the Groundwork

Over those three weeks, we send out a ton of relevant worksheets and questionnaires to get people ready for working with us. We also talk very openly about where they'll get support, so clients know exactly what to expect and what's expected of them. This lays the groundwork for a trusting, rock-solid relationship and total clarity when our work together finally begins.

B: Make Sure Things Are Crystal Clear

We check in often in the beginning to see if anyone has questions, and we have a customer support team there to make sure everyone gets what she needs.

C: Set Boundaries

Being clear with new clients about how available you're going to be is the key to avoiding overwhelm. For example, we'll tell new clients to please wait twenty-four hours for a response from us if they run into any trouble, and a little longer if they contact us on a weekend. We will absolutely respond, but setting this precedent helps us avoid panicked "I've waited three hours for a response!" popping up over and over.

Now it's your turn to create a sequence that supports your new clients. These questions will help you get started, and you can use the space provided to start answering them!

Purchase Sequence

How will your clients purchase something from you? Etsy? PayPal? E-junkie? What happens after they make their purchase? Will they receive an auto-responder email from you? Will you respond to each purchase individually? Will you have to package something and bring it to the post office?

What legalities do you need to cover when someone makes a purchase? Do you need to send her a nondisclosure agreement? A noncompete statement? A disclaimer? How will you send her any legal documents?

Nurture Sequence

What information do you need from you clients before you start working with them? If you're sending them a physical product, do you need any sizing or color preference information? Is there any information you can send them before you start working together that will help make your work go more smoothly?

How can you make sure your clients are totally ready and informed before you start working together?

What boundaries do you want to set with your client work? Will you answer emails in the evening or weekends? How long does it take for you to return emails? Are there any topics that are off limits? Do you have a rush fee? Do you have a limited number of edits?

Now let's transfer the information from these tables to the following chart. This will help you solidify your process.

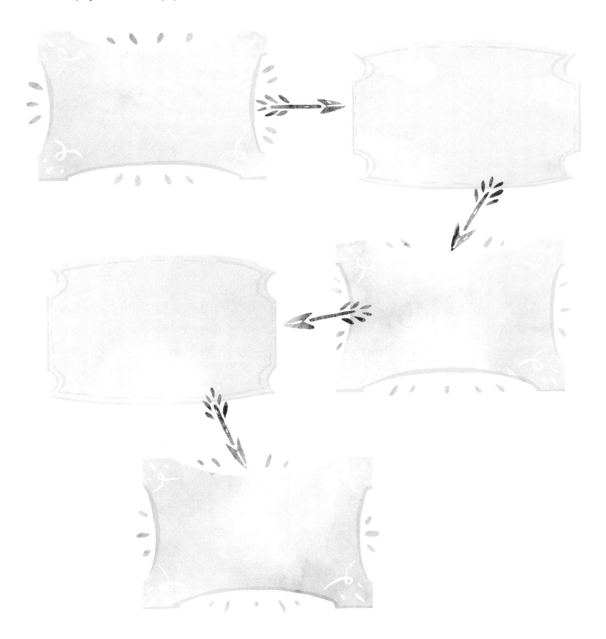

PILLAR 4: The Right Accounting Process

Spreadsheets and budgeting might not be your idea of a good time, but I bet you enjoy having a bit of extra cash for a winter vacation somewhere beachy or a new pair of shoes, right?

It's significantly easier to book that flight and pack your swimsuit when you've created a basic accounting system. When you create simple systems around accounting and your finances, you're empowering yourself to make the smartest decisions for your business. I want to (lovingly) shine a big flashlight onto your accounting process, finances, and how you think about your money. We'll dive deeper into all things money in the next step of *The Conquer Kit* and you'll create a budget on page 166.

For now, I want you to start thinking about your accounting process. If you don't have an accounting process already, you're running your business in the dark, but I promise to guide you to the light. I highly recommend speaking with an accountant about your current and future accounting process because this is a system that will be highly personal to you, the type of business you run, and the reporting requirements you have in your country and region.

On the next page you'll see an illustration of how I handle my accounting.

I SEND ALL MY RECEIPTS TO SHOEBOXED TO BE SCANNED AND ORGANIZED INTO CATEGORIES

MY ACCOUNTANT DOES AN EXPORT FROM SHOEBOXED TO QUICKBOOKS ONLINE

WE USE QUICKBOOKS TO KEEP ON TOP OF OUR BOOKS AND RUN OUR PAYROLL

MY ACCOUNTANT GENERATES KEY FINANCIAL STATEMENTS FOR ME AND CREATES A REPORT EACH MONTH SO I'M EMPOWERED TO MAKE SMART DECISIONS

Your Financial Check-Up

⏱ **15 MINUTES**

If dollars and cents aren't your strong suit, it's hard to know how to even begin when it's time to piece together your money systems.

Luckily, I've come up with a super simple solution. Use the following flowchart to figure out what kind of financial systems your business needs and where you should be taking steps today.

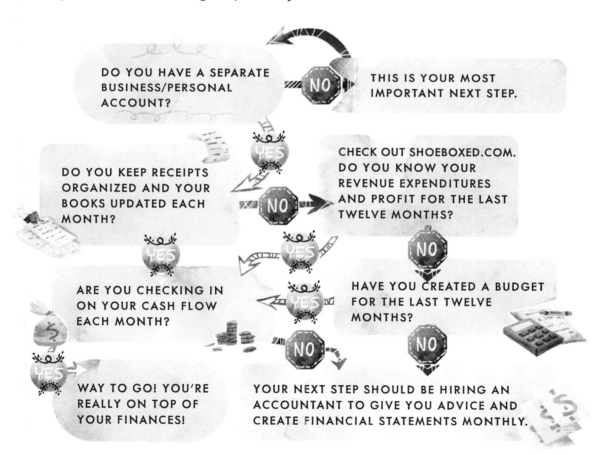

DO YOU HAVE A SEPARATE BUSINESS/PERSONAL ACCOUNT?

NO → THIS IS YOUR MOST IMPORTANT NEXT STEP.

YES ↓

DO YOU KEEP RECEIPTS ORGANIZED AND YOUR BOOKS UPDATED EACH MONTH?

NO → CHECK OUT SHOEBOXED.COM. DO YOU KNOW YOUR REVENUE EXPENDITURES AND PROFIT FOR THE LAST TWELVE MONTHS?

YES ↓

NO →

YES ↓

ARE YOU CHECKING IN ON YOUR CASH FLOW EACH MONTH?

HAVE YOU CREATED A BUDGET FOR THE LAST TWELVE MONTHS?

YES ↓

NO →

NO →

WAY TO GO! YOU'RE REALLY ON TOP OF YOUR FINANCES!

YOUR NEXT STEP SHOULD BE HIRING AN ACCOUNTANT TO GIVE YOU ADVICE AND CREATE FINANCIAL STATEMENTS MONTHLY.

A Treasure Chest of Tools for Stress-Free Accounting

If you want to be (and stay) in loving control of your business's finances, it helps to make friends with a few handy people and pieces of technology that I recommend you take a look at as you create the right accounting system for you.

Hiring a bookkeeper: Bookkeepers are worth their weight in gold. Having a certified brain in your corner who can give you basic financial advice, even if you're just starting out, will do wonders for the financial stability (and future) of your business.

QuickBooks, Wave Accounting, and Xero: These handy digital tools are the simplest, cleanest way to manage your finances, from invoices to payroll and tax reports. You can use their smartphone or desktop apps from anywhere and get access to all your financial data in one place.

FreshBooks: A favorite among service providers, this is one of the top options for tracking your time and invoicing online. FreshBooks also allows you to accept credit card payments right away, right from the invoice.

inDinero: Created by a whip-smart young woman who's now a rising star in Silicon Valley, this is a robust solution for a growing business that's scaling really quickly. It's got everything you need to manage your corporate tax returns, payroll, and more.

Shoeboxed: In terms of organizing receipts, this nifty little app has changed my life and probably saved me thousands of dollars. No matter where I am in the world, I can take a picture of a receipt or I can send in all my paper receipts in an envelope, and the Shoeboxed team will organize them so my accountant can export them to QuickBooks. Note: Check with your country's jurisdiction and make sure you're allowed to use digital receipts when you're reporting your finances!

Building the pillars to a successful business isn't always sexy or swing-from-the-rafters fun, but you did it, Conqueror! You created a name that resonates with you and future customers and laid a bit of legal groundwork. You worked to familiarize yourself with systems that will save you time and money, and you learned about the art of accounting.

This groundwork will pay off—exponentially—down the road. Your future business thanks you!

4

STEP 4

Get Your Mind on Your Money

Successful people make money.
It's not that people who make money
become successful, but that successful
people attract money. They bring success
to what they do.

— WAYNE DYER

STEP 4: GET YOUR MIND ON YOUR MONEY

Many, many of us have been led to believe that talking about money is crass and wanting more of it is tacky or selfish. If this is an idea you hold, I'm here to tell you:

1. It's not true.
2. You have permission to let go of that thought process.

Money is like electricity—it's neither good nor bad, but it can certainly be used for both. Think of all the amazing things you could do if you had a bit more of it! Start scholarships, build schools in developing countries, or send your parents on a nice cruise.

Have I convinced you? Even entrepreneurs who care more about making meaning than making money need to understand their finances in order to make the best decisions and build the business of their dreams.

Do you know:

- How much income you earned last month?

- How much you paid out in expenses?

- How to read your financial statements to make decisions as an entrepreneur?

If you do, awesome! If not, I'm going to help you feel empowered when it comes to your money. Budget sheets? Cash flow statements? Profit and loss? We're going to lift the curtain on all things related to your business finances in this step of *The Conquer Kit*.

Soulful Money Rituals

ⓧ **20 MINUTES**

What's an easy, heartfelt way to approach and shift your mindset around money? How can you release the stress and confusion that arises when, say, you're reviewing or creating your budget for the year?

The answer: developing your own rituals and habits around money.

Look at it this way: Creating rituals (of any kind!) is a deeply personal and incredibly rewarding experience—so why not create a few around money? They will help you focus on finances from a place of soul-centered clarity.

For example, I have a daily gratitude practice around money. When I receive money, I say thank you to the person and the powers that be in the universe. By doing so, I'm honoring what that influx of money means for me, my business, and my purpose on this planet.

I also organize bills and bank statements as they come in because it throws me off my game if I enter my office in the morning and immediately see a cluttered pile of bills and financial paperwork that I've been ignoring. It makes my heart space contract and feel tight, and that's no way to kick off a day.

It's very important to get into a practice of consciously honoring and being grateful for your money. If you're repaying debt, it's even important to have a gratitude practice around that.

Send that grace on up: "Thank you for allowing me to make another payment toward this debt, and I trust that it will be gone at some point."

The feng shui of my finances is also another wealth practice I have in place. For example, I'm very selective about what I spend my money on and I don't like pouring dollars into stuff and clutter that can block the flow of energy in other parts of my world. I consciously invest in quality over quantity. I want great design in all of my programs and a beautifully responsive and sleek website. These are things that also help me offer more value to my clients and customers.

I encourage you to look at symbols and objects that represent prosperity and abundance in different cultures. Flowing water, crystals, koi fish imagery—all of these can be used to supercharge your money mindset, and transform your thinking around profit as a necessary evil into a blessed form of energy.

What makes you think "I am prosperous and accumulating wealth" when you look at it? Create your own mantra and attach it to objects that are meaningful to you. Having that ritual in your life creates a strong energy that magnetizes more money to you.

Don't believe me? Try it for yourself! See what happens.

Write your own mantra for money:

What objects are financially meaningful to you?

What stressful money practices could you let go of?

Lifting the Financial Curtain

It's time to get your financial house in order! My CFO and a Conquer Club money mentor, Julia Jenner, played a significant part in creating this section of the book, and I am eternally grateful for her contribution so I could equip you with the fundamental knowledge you need to craft a clear picture of your current financial situation and demystify the financials in your business. We want you to feel empowered when it comes to your money, and if you didn't go to business school, there's a chance the numbers in your business terrify you.

Understanding and tracking finances is a struggle for many entrepreneurs— especially creatives. It doesn't have to be painful or complicated though. Trust me! That's why we included this section for you.

Simply put: Your business needs systems in place for ingoing and outgoing money.

And, on a spiritual level, if you have a system for receiving money and that is organized and clean, it invites abundance. Money is energy. It all goes back to flow. If your financial life is a complete mess, and you can't pull out receipts or have certain key documents at the ready, you're creating heaps of obstacles for yourself that can get in the way of prosperity and create pathways for chaos.

For now, let's put all that anxiety around numbers and budget sheets aside and focus on the basics that every entrepreneur needs to know.

Managing your core financial system means keeping diligent track of all of your invoices, expenses, receipts, and more.

Here are a few questions you should be asking yourself as you start your organization process:

- When do your invoices go out?

- What are you taking as a deposit versus a final payment?

- When do customers pay you?

- Do you have a separate credit card for business expenses?

- Are you going to use PayPal or Square, or accept checks?

This is all must-know information!

But I get it: While invoices are easier to monitor, it's hard to keep track of every single receipt and expense, right? Especially if you travel often or have a massive purse that acts as a black hole!

Fortunately, there's a really easy way to keep your expenses orderly: It's called Shoeboxed, and I briefly mentioned it earlier. This handy little app helps me store and manage all of my receipts electronically, and allows me to export those receipts to QuickBooks so my accountant can keep our books updated and create financial statements for me.

"Hold up. What are these financial statements you say I need, Natalie?"

In accountant terms, financial statements record the financial activities of a business or the financial effects of doing business. In normal human terms, they're a map that tells you where your money came from, where it went, and where it is now. Simple!

Later, we'll translate the different parts of your monthly financial statements. But before we start, I'd like you to promise me something, dear Conqueror. If you don't already read your financial statements on a regular basis, I want you to promise to read this section—no skipping, no skimming. And I promise you in return that I'll explain everything as simply as I can and then we'll dive into the stuff that Conquerors find more fun than systems and finances.

I know this financial stuff can seem boring or overwhelming, but when you understand your money, you're more powerful and better informed. You arrive in a magical place where you can make better decisions about your business.

You might be wondering where to get these financial statements I'm talking about.

Fun fact: You do not need your accountant to draw up an official set of financial statements each month anymore, thanks to some awesome tools available to you. I'll include some recommendations; however, you should check out tools you know you can use in your country. Your bookkeeper or your bookkeeping software can hook you up with all the reports you need:

- A profit and loss account (also known as an income statement) for the month that details each individual transaction

- A profit and loss account on a month-by-month basis

- A profit and loss account that compares your actual results for the month versus budget

- A balance sheet

Your Income Statement

Your income statement tells you where your money came from and where it went. You can look at income statements for specific periods of time—a week, a month, a quarter, or the whole year.

At the top of your income statement you'll find your sales revenue, below that you'll find expenses. The literal bottom line is your net profit or loss (sometimes called net income).

Just remember: revenue at the top, expenses in the middle, profit at the bottom.

Expenses include things like office supplies, software, and subcontractor costs—costs required to run your business.

Expenses should not include your salary (unless you are on an official payroll) or income taxes (which are often dealt with through the owner's personal income statement).

ETERNITY ECO-FASHION / INCOME STATEMENT

December 2015

	Dec 15	
Ordinary Income/Expense		
Income		
Retail Sales	28,467.31	
Custom Designs	1,700.00	**REVENUE**
Total Income	30,167.31	
Cost of Goods Sold		
Cost of Goods Sold	14,832.97	
Total COGS	14,832.97	
Gross Profit	15,334.34	
Expense		
Automobile	367.29	
Insurance	467.04	
Interest Expense	146.61	**EXPENSES**
Payroll Expenses	6,299.11	
Rent	3,750.00	
Utilities	670.80	
Total Expense	11,700.85	
Net Ordinary Income	3,633.49	
Net Income	**3,633.49**	**PROFIT**

The Balance Sheet

The balance sheet is a snapshot on a particular day of your business's assets (what it owns or controls, its cash and inventory), liabilities (what you owe other people), and owner's equity (what you, the owner, are owed!). These sheets are mostly used to show what's happening at the end of a particular month or year.

By focusing on what you currently own and comparing them to what you owe other people, you'll be able to determine your ability to pay upcoming bills and to finance growth.

ETERNITY ECO-FASHION / BALANCE SHEET

	Dec 31, 15
ASSETS	
Current Assets	
Checking/Savings	
Checking	3,613.01
Savings	30,757.70
Petty Cash	510.00
Total Checking/Savings	34,880.70
Other Current Assets	
Inventory Asset	5,113.90
Total Other Current Assets	5,113.90
Total Current Assets	39,994.60
Fixed Assets	
Furniture and Equipment	11,442.00
Total Fixed Assets	11,442.00
TOTAL ASSETS	51,436.60
LIABILITIES & EQUITY	
Liabilities	
Current Liabilities	
Accounts Payable	
Accounts Payable	2,048.99
Total Accounts Payable	2,048.99
Credit Cards	
Credit Card	382.62
Total Credit Cards	382.62
Other Current Liabilities	
Payroll Liabilities	415.73
Sales Tax Payable	136.80
Total Other Current Liabilities	552.53
Total Current Liabilities	2,984.14
Total Liabilities	2,984.14
Equity	
Capital Stock	100.00
Retained Earnings	4,750.57
Net Income	43,601.88
Total Equity	48,452.45
TOTAL LIABILITIES & EQUITY	51,436.60

OWNED

OWED TO OTHER PEOPLE

OWED TO OWNER

Your Transactional Profit and Loss Account

Browse your profit and loss account, an in-depth transaction sheet, to check for entries that:

- You were not expecting

- Look wrong

- Are misclassified (for example, personal expenses)

ETERNITY ECO-FASHION / TRANSACTIONAL PROFIT + LOSS

	Invoice	12/24/2015 1962	Daily Till Receipts	Checking	1,972.48	23,678.13
	Invoice	12/27/2015 1963	Daily Till Receipts	Checking	1,044.25	24,722.38
	Invoice	12/28/2015 1964	Daily Till Receipts	Checking	1,102.27	25,824.65
	Invoice	12/29/2015 1965	Daily Till Receipts	Checking	905.02	26,729.67
	Invoice	12/30/2015 1966	Daily Till Receipts	Checking	1,086.02	27,815.69
	Invoice	12/31/2015 1967	Daily Till Receipts	Checking	651.61	28,467.31
Total Retail Sales					28,467.31	28,467.31
Custom Designs						
	Invoice	12/01/2015 251	Moyra Murron	Checking	450.00	450.00
	Invoice	12/03/2015 252	Edna Innes	Checking	600.00	1,050.00
	Invoice	12/17/2015 253	Aileen Marsaili	Checking	650.00	1,700.00
Total Custom Designs					1,700.00	1,700.00
Total Income					**30,167.31**	**30,167.31**
Cost of Goods Sold						
Cost of Goods Sold						
	Invoice	12/01/2015 794	Parkway Designs	Accounts Payable	969.85	969.85
	Invoice	12/02/2015 185-236	Eco-Eco	Accounts Payable	342.30	1,312.15
	Invoice	12/02/2015 C475	Summit Clothing	Accounts Payable	570.50	,882.65
	Invoice	12/04/2015 INV-0108	Violet & Viola	Accounts Payable	627.55	2,510.19

A Month-by-Month Profit and Loss Account

Review your month-by-month profit and loss account for your net profit (or loss). In other words, we're looking for the return on your efforts. Your overriding goal as a business owner is to earn more from customers in sales than you pay out to suppliers and employees in costs.

ETERNITY ECO-FASHION / MONTHLY PROFIT + LOSS

	Sep 15	Oct 15	Nov 15	Dec 15
Ordinary Income/Expense				
Income				
Retail Sales	34,075.37	17,934.41	17,080.39	28,467.31
Custom Designs	525.00	0.00	1,175.00	1,700.00
Total Income	34,600.37	17,934.41	18,255.39	30,167.31
Cost of Goods Sold				
Cost of Goods Sold	17,646.19	8,967.20	8,762.59	14,832.97
Total COGS	17,646.19	8,967.20	8,762.59	14,832.97
Gross Profit	16,954.18	8,967.21	9,492.80	15,334.34
Expense				
Advertising	2,450.00	0.00	1,329.80	0.00
Automobile	251.23	209.36	220.37	367.29
Bank Service Charges	0.00	70.00	0.00	0.00
Insurance	467.04	0.00	0.00	467.04
Interest Expense	151.05	149.56	148.08	146.61
Legal & Professional	0.00	750.00	0.00	0.00
Payroll Expenses	5,588.70	5,272.36	5,669.20	6,299.11
Rent	3,750.00	0.00	0.00	3,750.00
Utilities	696.20	156.43	192.12	670.80
Total Expense	13,354.22	6,607.71	7,559.57	11,700.85
Net Ordinary Income	3,599.97	2,359.50	1,933.23	3,633.49
Net Income	**3,599.96**	**2,359.50**	**1,933.23**	**3,633.49**

If the profit you've made isn't enough to meet your needs, review your sales and costs and see where you can make changes.

Look for trends in your monthly income and expenses. Does anything stand out like a sore thumb—because it's higher or lower than normal? Do you know why those numbers are different from what you'd expect?

Review the money you're spending and consider why you're spending it. What are the results of spending that money?

- How many people bought your book because of that Facebook ad?

- How much did you spend hosting that workshop? How much money did you make on the workshop?

- How much are you paying your team? How much money are you making each month?

- How many people signed up for your newsletter because you advertised on a targeted site?

This spending should have a purpose that can be measured. It's less scary to spend money when you know where it's going and how it will positively affect your business.

What You Budgeted Versus What Actually Happened

Now let's compare your budget to what actually happened. How much revenue did you actually earn compared to what you expected? And how much did you spend versus what you budgeted?

ETERNITY ECO-FASHION / BUDGET VS ACTUAL

	Dec 15	Budget	$ Over Budget
Ordinary Income/Expense			
Income			
Retail Sales	28,467.31	25,000.00	3,467.31
Custom Designs	1,700.00	2,000.00	-300.00
Total Income	30,167.31	27,000.00	3,167.31
Cost of Goods Sold			
Cost of Goods Sold	14,832.97	13,500.00	1,332.97
Total COGS	14,832.97	13,500.00	1,332.97
Gross Profit	15,334.34	13,500.00	1,834.34
Expense			
Automobile	367.29	350.00	17.29
Insurance	467.04	467.04	0.00
Interest Expense	146.61	150.00	-3.39
Payroll Expenses	6,299.11	5,670.00	629.11
Rent	3,750.00	3,750.00	0.00
Utilities	670.80	700.00	-29.20
Total Expense	11,700.85	11,087.04	613.81
Net Ordinary Income	3,633.49	2,412.96	1,220.54
Net Income	**3,633.49**	**2,412.96**	**1,220.54**

When you're looking at your budget, think about those unexpected moments. Surely, some unexpected moments were good (when your product was featured on a huge blog and you got hundreds of new customers) and some things were less great (when everyone spent their money on the holidays and couldn't afford your services). Examine those unexpected moments when your budget veered from its expected path.

- **Good differences** (when you unexpectedly made more money)

- **Bad differences** (when you made less money than expected)

- **Timing differences** (when you thought you'd be paid or charged on a certain date and weren't)

Think about why this happened. Is there anything you can do about these unexpected moments? Could you require that clients pay when they book their sessions with you? Could you create a bigger inventory so you won't be left high and dry when there's a run on your products? Could you have a sale next January?

The Balance Sheet

Confirm that your bank, credit card, and PayPal balances match up with your statements. If they don't, find out why and correct the differences.

Review your cash balances. Cash is the lifeblood of any business, so manage it wisely. Do you have enough cash to pay off your credit card balances and any other short-term liabilities? Do you have enough cash for your future plans? Consult your budget to check your expected net cash flows for the next few months.

Work out how you are going to cover any shortfalls.

As you get more comfortable with the financial side of your business, it'll become easier and faster. Once you're experienced, it might only take you half an hour a month. That half an hour will help you take huge strides toward your financial goals!

How Do You Get All This Information?

Ideally you have a bookkeeper who (lovingly) hassles you at the start of each month to send in your financial information and sends over the reports we talked about earlier. You can also do it yourself with tools like Wave Accounting or Xero.

These tools allow you to pull in feeds from your bank and credit card accounts. But if you've got a more complex financial situation (your transactions are in multiple currencies, for example), I'd really recommend finding a professional bookkeeper.

A Check to Your Future Self

⏱ **5 MINUTES**

How are you feeling about your money now? Can you imagine your future self looking at financial statements that show the millions of dollars flowing into your business? One of my favorite ways to keep my mind on my money and my financial goals is by writing my future self a check for the amount I'd like to be able to cash by a certain date. I think it's a perfect (and fun!) exercise to wrap up this step with.

Think about how much money you'd like to have twelve months from now. Fill out the check below or tear a check out of your checkbook and paste it below.

YOUR NAME Your Address Your City, State, Zip Code	Date _____

Pay to The
Order of _____ **$** [   ]

_____ **Dollars**

Authorized
Signature _____   Memo _____

1234 - 567898765 - 4321234

5

Sell Your Soul

(aka Heart-Centric Marketing)

People don't buy what you do,
they buy why you do it.

— SIMON SINEK

STEP 5: SELL YOUR SOUL (AKA HEART-CENTRIC MARKETING)

Do you hear the words *sales and marketing* and cringe? Die a little inside? Roll your eyes and devoutly hope that your product is so good you won't have to do any of that dirty marketing business?

If this sounds familiar, you're not alone. So many people (especially women and creative types, dare I say) are reticent about marketing and sales. But really, marketing is nothing other than sharing the story behind your company and brand and telling your customers about your products and why they might like them. And it's possible to do that without dry press release templates or tacky, blinking "Buy Now!" buttons.

When you create products and services that are helpful, useful, and fulfill a need, you don't need all the cheesy bells and whistles. Marketing can take the form of gorgeous photos or sharing the inspiration behind any given product. Marketing can look like funny product descriptions or short, honest emails telling your friends and followers that you've got space in your class and, if they're interested, you'd love to have them.

I'm going to help you create a blueprint for your website, develop compelling copy and sound bites for the media, get gorgeous testimonials from your raving clients, and feel more confident about selling than ever before. Even better? I'll teach you how to do all that while still being *true to you*.

Give, Give, Give

⏱ **30 MINUTES**

Most of us don't like sales and marketing because we hate asking for things—asking for the sale, asking for the retweet, asking for the meeting.

But there's a really easy way to get around that: give, give, give before you ask for anything. Give tons of helpful advice in your blog posts and videos. Give incredible ebooks to the people who sign up for your list—and then give them discounts on your offerings. Give traffic to people you like by sharing their work on your blog and social media. Give advice to newbies by speaking at conferences and taking part in telesummits.

When you're generous with your time and talents, people notice. And all that giving you've done? You've shown people that you're a kind, helpful, likable expert—just the type of person they want to hire when the time comes.

WHAT I WANT: MORE TRAFFIC

Three ways I can be generous and send traffic to other people:

WHAT I WANT: MORE LIST SIGN-UPS

Three ways I can be generous with my readers that will reward them for signing up:

WHAT I WANT: MORE SALES

Three ways I can be generous that will lead to more sales:

Customers As Your Storytellers and Sales Team

⏱ ONGOING

It's OK (and even encouraged!) to toot your own horn. But it can be just as effective to let other people do the talking.

One of the most effective sales tools you have is your list of satisfied clients. Now is the time to reach out and ask them what, exactly, they liked about you and your products.

If you're a service provider, send your clients a feedback form the second you wrap up your work together. If you create physical products, send a follow-up email when you know your customers have received it and had a chance to try it out. You can also include a thank-you note with their purchase and offer them a discount on their next purchase if they fill out your feedback form.

Don't be afraid to ask your clients for specifics—if you know Mark's Twitter presence increased exponentially after working with you, ask him to highlight that. If you know Dana lost thirty-five pounds due to your products, ask her to address that in her testimonial. Try to diversify your testimonials so each of them addresses a different aspect of your product or offering.

It's also good to ask your clients why they needed your help and if they needed to overcome any doubts before they hired you. If someone's doubtful about working with a life coach, for instance, they're more likely to hire you if you have a testimonial that reads "I was extremely skeptical about life coaches—until I hired Lisa."

Client name: _____

Product used: _____

Aspect of product I think they liked best: _____

Date I emailed them asking for a testimonial: _____

Client name: _____

Product used: _____

Aspect of product I think they liked best: _____

Date I emailed them asking for a testimonial: _____

Client name: _____

Product used: _____

Aspect of product I think they liked best: _____

Date I emailed them asking for a testimonial: _____

Client name: _____

Product used: _____

Aspect of product I think they liked best: _____

Date I emailed them asking for a testimonial: _____

Conquer a Year of Content in a Day

⏱ **FULL DAY**

In this day and age, nothing helps you sell your heart out like incredible content. When you consistently give heaps of value through the content you share, selling feels a lot less icky, which is a feeling a lot of us would love to banish forever when it comes to sales. The key here is consistency.

I create a weekly video to send my audience, and these videos are at the heart of our content marketing strategy. Generosity is one of our core values at She Takes on the World Inc., so we also offer free events, worksheets, and trainings. When you're generous, people notice. And all that giving you've done? You've shown people that you're a kind, helpful, likable expert with good intentions—just the type of person they want to hire when the time comes. When we open the doors to the Conquer Club each year, selling feels good because we provide consistent value all year long.

Now, do you think I sit down once every week to create my weekly video? No, I don't. With my busy schedule and the amount of traveling I do, it just wouldn't be possible to film in my studio each week. Instead, I batch my filming so I film multiple episodes in one or two days. That way, we always have a four-month content calendar that allows us to see what's coming up next. We can schedule emails and social media updates to go out too.

I want to let you in on a big secret: I once created fifty pieces of content in one day, pretty much a whole year of content. And that brings me to your next mission.

Below is the process I use for filling up my content calendar, and creating loads of valuable content in one sitting, and it's your next mission:

1. Visit your Facebook page or send out an email and crowd-source questions, comments, pain points, challenges, and suggestions from your audience. What questions do they ask that you have an answer to?

2. Organize this feedback into a list, and don't hesitate to add a few of your own ideas in there. I've found that reading through my audience's feedback really gets my ideas flowing, too.

3. Now go through and write a few talking points that you will use to answer each question on the list.

4. Next, download an app like SuperNote Recorder, and record yourself answering the questions. Or you can turn on your webcam and film your responses if you want to create video content. You can also hire a videographer if you want to go a step above the webcam, but we all start somewhere. Before I hired my production team, it was just me and my webcam for episodes of She Takes on the World TV.

5. Go through question by question and make sure you hit on the key talking points you wanted to share.

6. When you're done filming, you or an editor can edit the individual videos, and voilà, you have video blogs ready to go. Or, if you're creating written content you can send the recordings off to a transcriptionist. You can find transcribers at the ready on Upwork, and when the transcript comes back you just have to edit your responses to finalize your written content.

The last step is to schedule the release dates for all the content you created. This is your content calendar! Now you can also create email blasts, social media updates, and graphics for your content. Consider yourself ahead of the game now, Conqueror.

How much content were you able to create for this mission? Let me know @nataliemacneil.

Board of Advisers Meditation

⏱ 20 MINUTES

Being an entrepreneur means making lots of decisions—lots. You need to know when it's time to step into warrior mode and when it's time to pull back a bit and nurture yourself and your body. There are also some entrepreneurial hats that you may not feel comfortable wearing, like Head of Sales or Financial Maven.

When I find myself in uncomfortable situations, I use my Board of Advisers meditation. It's a simple, loving way to examine all sides of a situation and step into a different mental space. You can listen to the audio version of this meditation at shetakesontheworld.com/conquerkitbonuses.

Here's how it works: I want you to visualize yourself sitting in a boardroom with all the people who really inspire you. They can be close friends or family, your heroes from history (alive or dead), even fictional characters. Full disclosure: I have Daenerys Targaryen from *Game of Thrones* in my boardroom as my Queen adviser. Amelia Earhart is in my boardroom too. She's someone I admire for the risks she took to pursue dreams that people didn't think were even possible for women at the time.

Think of people who align with the other Conqueror archetypes, and cut and paste photos of your own board members on the next page.

During the meditation, focus on the person who would be best suited to advise your current situation and home in on her energy. Focus on the qualities she has that you need to develop. Visualize a ball of light transferring from her heart to yours, and all those qualities you admire in that person are now within you too. Imagine yourself embodying her power and her gifts.

Examine your mindset after that meditation. Are you seeing the situation any differently?

After you come out of the meditation and navigate the challenge you're facing, continue to embody that person's energy. While it may feel like you're playing a part at first, with a little practice, you'll actually train yourself to embody that strength mindset each time you encounter a challenge. And really, the gifts, qualities, and light you value in another person are a reflection of you.

YOUR BOARD OF ADVISERS

Cut and paste pictures of your dream advisory team below:

Your Cover Story

⏱ **1 HOUR**

Time and time again, I come across entrepreneurs (especially women) who just don't feel comfortable owning their gifts. They worry about bragging, or sounding insincere, or alienating people.

I get it. Some of us struggle to share our accomplishments without feeling like egotistical jerks. But there is a key difference between sounding conceited and calmly, confidently letting people know where your power lies and how you're changing the world with your work.

To navigate the difference between confidence and conceited, we're going to pretend a bit. Let's pull out our (imaginary) press passes and write a feature story about you and your business for an imaginary publication. But, you're not writing the article as yourself. Instead, imagine you're a third party interviewing you about your work. Imagine this piece is for an audience who has never heard of you or what you do.

The key here is to captivate and wow them, while describing your work in the simplest, most engaging way possible. Tall order? Yes. But I know you're up to it! Ready? Write all about it on the next page!

Your Story

PHOTO HERE

Brand Vibe Board

⏱ **2 TO 3 HOURS TO START + ONGOING PROCESS**

If you're not quite sure which direction you'd like to take your brand, a brand vibe board can help you gain serious clarity about the overall tone and visual vibe of your business.

Back when I was working with my web strategist on a rebrand for SheTakesOnTheWorld.com, we created my own Brand Vibe Board. It included my logo, color scheme, patterns, and images that felt like my brand, along with the best shots from my photoshoot, fonts we loved, and more. It helped me make sure every choice we made—the copy, the headshots, the social media icons—worked together to create an online space my audience—and I!—loved.

We could double-check every choice we made against that board so we'd stay on track and stay true to our vision.

Now, in this exercise, it's your turn!

If you're building your brand from scratch or you're shooting for a rebrand, this exercise may take a little longer than if you already have a strong sense of your brand. Be patient with yourself, but stay focused on how you want your work to look and feel out there in the virtual realm.

You can also give this Brand Vibe Board to your designer as a starting point for gorgeous graphics and a website you love. Ready to get started? Have a dig through magazines and flyers and pull images and font choices that you like, or even turns of phrase you enjoy. Don't worry too much or analyze if something works with your brand—if it speaks to you, rip it out!

Once you've gathered inspiration, snap a photo of your Brand Vibe Board so you can send it to a designer. While you're at it, share it with me on Instagram @nataliemacneil. Of course, if you're more of an online girl, Pinterest is a great place to build a digital Brand Vibe Board, although I'm a paper girl at heart and always like starting things on paper first.

LOGO

TYPOGRAPHY (FONTS)

PATTERNS & GRAPHICS

ICONS

Your Website Blueprint

Your website is your digital home, and if built right, it can be one of the most powerful tools you have for driving sales.

Complete the blueprint below, and then book some time with your web developer to ensure this blueprint is built into your digital home.

How do people get to your website? Social media, advertising, search engine results, directly from the URL you share?

What action do you ask visitors to take when they arrive at your website? Schedule a free demo, book a consultation, claim a discount or free offer?

How do you nurture leads generated through your website? Free resources, valuable content shared on your blog and social media, events?

How do you elegantly sell? Product video, beautiful sales page, copy that connects to the hearts of your potential customers?

WEBSITE MUST-HAVES:

- ☐ A homepage description that tells visitors who you are and what you do
- ☐ Calls to action that let your visitors know what they should do next
- ☐ Mobile responsive design
- ☐ Your contact information
- ☐ A map and directions if you have a physical location
- ☐ An opt-in offer for capturing leads
- ☐ Product or service pages that convert leads into paying customers
- ☐ Web analytics tools, like Google Analytics, to track key data about your traffic and conversion rates

Message Clarity Microscope

⏱ **20 MINUTES**

Want to develop your brand and overall messaging to use on your website and marketing materials? This exercise will help you do just that, in two condensed steps. This exercise was created and contributed by my friend and copywriter Hillary Weiss, and it's a great way to pull together awesome phrasing you can use in your copy.

This is, at its core, a self-interview experience. You'll answer some insightful, thought-provoking questions, record your responses, and take notes on how these answers resonate with you and reflect your goals. Let's dig in!

You'll need:

- Something to record with (Your laptop or smartphone probably has a program/app for this already. Can't find it? Try Vocaroo, the online audio recorder.)

- A timer set for twenty minutes

PART 1: Hit "Record"

Spend twenty minutes answering the following questions with as much or as little information as feels right. Let yourself speak freely and get passionate and fired up if that's how you really feel!

Be as specific as possible. If you hear yourself speaking in vague, blanket terms ("I want to help people be happier"; "I want my clients to lose weight"), go deeper ("I want to teach my clients about nourishing themselves in every aspect of their lives").

Question 1

What road got you to where you are now in your work? Where did you begin? What does your present look like? What's ahead for you?

Question 2

Who exactly are you speaking to? What's your prospective client struggling with on the surface? On a deeper, more subconscious level, where is she struggling?

Question 3

Why do you l-o-v-e your work? Why do you find this work inspiring?

Question 4

What results will your clients see? How will these results affect them—next week, next month, next year . . . even twenty years from now?

Question 5

List the adjectives you'd like to see at the end of this sentence:

When people work with me, they feel _____.

For example, here's how I'd answer this question: "When people work with me, they feel inspired, more knowledgeable, ready for what's next, and more grounded in their big-picture vision and goals."

PART 2: It's Note-Taking Time!

Give yourself a short break here—have a cup of tea, go for a short walk, work through a few yoga poses. All that talking can be a bit exhausting! Give your brain a bit of time to reboot.

When you're ready, play back the recording and jot down the best, most interesting bits.

Here are a few very specific things I want you to listen for:

- Phrases you hear yourself emphasizing or saying over and over again (for example, "I believe in _____" or "I'm all about _____"). These are hidden, handy one-liners you can make spicier with extra creative words or use as is. Either way, they can be put to work everywhere.

- The adjectives you use to describe your work and how you feel about it. These, or some jazzed-up synonyms, can become your signature buzzwords.

- How you talk about your clients' real needs. Have you ever experienced those needs yourself? Is their story your story too?

- The L factor. What do you hear yourself saying you love?

- Where you seem to hesitate or feel a little lost. Could this be a gap in your brand understanding? After you finish this exercise, take some time to really figure out what's missing and what you may need to explore further.

- The work-oriented stories you hear yourself telling—about your clients, your big vision, and so on. Everyone loves a good yarn, and you can use stories like this in blog posts, pitches, and sales pages galore.

Congratulations! You've successfully conducted a fabulous professional-level interview and unearthed some incredibly valuable insights.

6

STEP 6
Build an A-Team

Alone we can do so little,
together we can do so much.

— HELEN KELLER

STEP 6: BUILD AN A-TEAM

That old management chestnut is true—we're only as good as the people we surround ourselves with. If we're not careful, that can mean we're only as good as the deadline-missing assistant or the typo-creating graphic designer. But if we're clever and strategic, that means we're as good as our whip-smart social media consultant and as talented as our award-winning writer.

In this step, we'll talk about finding the right people to help you build your business—virtual assistants, designers, web developers, SEO consultants, and the list goes on. Even if you don't quite feel ready to hire people to work in your business, these exercises will help you determine who your first hire may be. We all need help, even if it's just hiring a virtual assistant for a few hours a week to take some of the busywork off your plate—things like scheduling, editing, email management, and other tasks that you don't need to be doing yourself. We'll also cover the interview questions you should ask before you hire someone (and tell you how to interview them). You don't have to do this alone, and you'll achieve more with a team than you ever could all by yourself.

Archetype Compatibility

⏱ 1 HOUR

When you're starting your search for a new brain for your business—whether it's a joint venture partner or a new team member—it's so, so easy to fall into the trap of hiring or partnering with someone just like you.

Why does this matter? When you hire or partner with someone similar to yourself, you might become great friends who share common interests, but you'll also probably share the same challenges and roadblocks.

Let's say you're a Dreamer archetype. You're fun-loving, super creative, and spend hours dreaming up ideas, but can have trouble with the follow-through. So, if you paired up with another Dreamer, not a whole lot is going to get done in your business, is it? It'll be a lot of fun and you'll probably have lots of phenomenal ideas together, but those ideas might not actually turn into much.

The Dreamer truly needs a Builder, and vice versa. The Builder's finely tuned mind can create the big vision; the Dreamer's vision is the blueprint the Builder needs.

To use a few more examples, the Queen needs someone like a Commander to direct her army (her team, systems, administrative details, etc.). A Revolutionary should *not* work with a Queen, as they almost always end up butting heads.

The Messenger is a great partner for most archetypes, particularly the Contributor, who needs the Messenger to help her rake in the currency most nonprofits deal in: visibility.

See what I mean?

To be clear: It's perfectly OK not to be fabulous at absolutely everything. No one's an expert at everything. Don't be afraid to play to your strengths!

In this exercise, you'll discover which archetype would make the best partner or team member for your obstacles and your wits.

> But please remember, if you're planning on working with a business partner long-term, a word of caution: Be very, very, very careful who you choose, if you choose anyone at all. While partnerships can be wonderful, it's very difficult to stay on the same page over months and years, and most partners will usually go their own way eventually.

First, write down your first and secondary archetypes:

My primary archetype: _____

My secondary archetype: _____

Now, write down your strengths, based on the archetypal description, your own experience, and the good feedback you get on your work.

My strengths are:

Hooray! You're clear on your strengths. Now, it's time to get radically, spectacularly honest with yourself and write down the areas you struggle with.

My challenges are:

Woo-hoo! You're clear about the places you need help and exactly what you need in a new partner or team member.

Based on the archetypes we listed in Step 1 (pages 28 – 31), write down which archetypes you feel would be the best fit for your needs:

Ideal archetype 1: _____

Ideal archetype 2: _____

Now that you know *who* you need, write down a few interview questions you should ask every potential team member or partner.

For example, if you're looking for a Builder, you can ask questions like these: Do you have experience launching products? How do you feel about team work? If you're looking for a Messenger, you can ask these kinds of questions: How do you feel about marketing? What's some of the best sales copy you've ever read?

Week-Long Time Audit

⏱ **1 WEEK**

When I'm deciding to make a new hire in my business, I always start with one big question: What am I spending the most time on that isn't growing revenue?

When I started out, I did everything myself. Every tweet, every edit, and every email—I dealt with them all. After a while, of course, it got to be too much. So what did I outsource first? Bookkeeping and accounting. While I know enough to make it work, receipts and tax deductions just aren't my areas of brilliance, and I was more than ready to hand that work over.

Why did I choose bookkeeping and accounting instead of, say, virtual assistant work (scheduling social media, uploading my blog posts, and posting YouTube videos)?

And the answer is weekly audits. Time audits, that is.

Here's how it works: Over seven days, I tracked what I was spending most of my time on. It was a great way to get a clear picture of where I was pouring my energy—and I was *floored* by how many hours I spent on things that weren't directly related to my message or work.

Now I want to help you do the same.

This exercise is designed to help you figure out what tasks can be outsourced and where you want to center more of your attention.

Your Mission

For the next week, I want you to track your time. You might be amazed at how much time you really, truly spend futzing around on social media or responding to emails!

There are two ways you can track your time: You can go old school or digital.

OLD SCHOOL

Set an alarm to ring every hour on the hour from 8 a.m. to 5 p.m. Each time that bell rings, write down what you've been working on.

You can use the chart on the next page to keep track.

	MONDAY	TUESDAY	WEDNESDAY	THURSDAY	FRIDAY
8 a.m.					
9 a.m.					
10 a.m.					
11 a.m.					
noon					
1 p.m.					
2 p.m.					
3 p.m.					
4 p.m.					
5 p.m.					

DIGITAL

Go to toggl.com and download their free time-tracking tool. Drag it into your toolbar and when you finish a task, track it. When you're finished, Toggl will even give you a pie chart of how you've spent your time!

Either of these methods will give you a better picture of where you should spend time and what you might want to look into hiring out or handing over to your existing team.

After the week is up, review each of the tasks you found yourself tackling and answer the following questions:

- What can you delegate?

- What do you want to spend more time on?

- What do you want to spend less time on?

- What can you delegate to your existing team?

The Team Hive

⏱ **1 HOUR**

All teams need guidance and motivation, but what you need from them can vary!

There are generally two types of business teams.

Physical teams. People who work alongside you in the same environment. Things to consider:

- You usually have to provide office space and equipment.

- You might spend more time micromanaging and interacting with team members than getting on with your own work.

Virtual teams. People who work for you but could be anywhere in the world. Things to consider:

- You need to trust them and feel confident in their ability to meet deadlines working on their own.

- Your communication must be crystal clear.

- You must stay on top of progress and be accessible if any questions or concerns arise.

Queen bee, it's time to build your hive.

In the honeycomb, write down your dream team member as well as the role you want her to play in your business.

THE TEAM HIVE

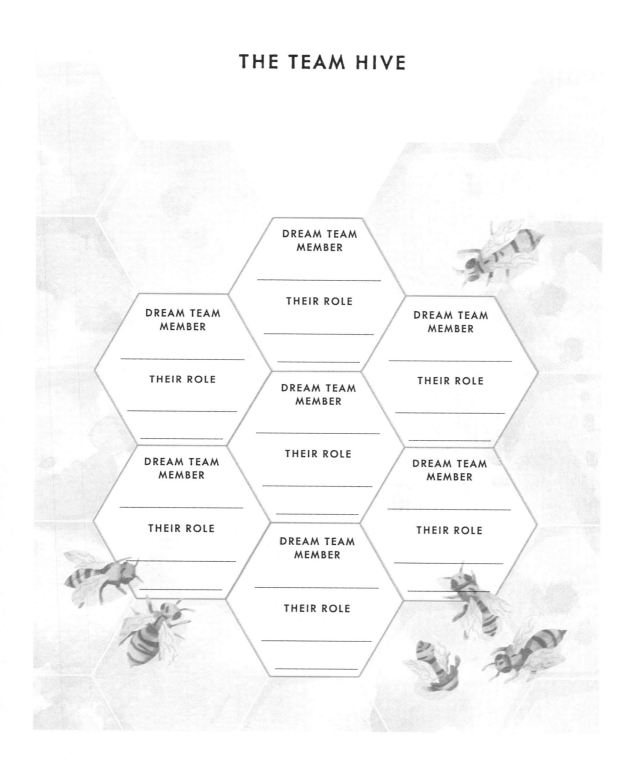

DREAM TEAM MEMBER

THEIR ROLE

DREAM TEAM MEMBER

THEIR ROLE

DREAM TEAM MEMBER

THEIR ROLE

DREAM TEAM MEMBER

THEIR ROLE

DREAM TEAM MEMBER

THEIR ROLE

DREAM TEAM MEMBER

THEIR ROLE

DREAM TEAM MEMBER

THEIR ROLE

Crafting Your Perfect Job Description

⏱ **45 MINUTES**

The hunt for the perfect team member or support can be a tricky one, especially if you're new to the game. But with the right job description, the best, most-qualified person will find *you*.

Personally, I've found most of my best team members through a mix of trusted referrals and experts from Upwork, but there are hundreds of resources out there that make it easy to post job listings and attract the dream team member you need.

While some entrepreneurs might suggest you outsource to countries like India for your systems and administrative tasks (you can easily hire overseas support for $2 to $4 an hour), I tend to take the opposite approach. Whether a team member is in NYC or Bangladesh, I always follow one rule: Pay fair wages. This is a personal stance I take in my business, but I certainly don't judge others for taking the lower-cost outsourcing path! However, I believe that when you pay people well, you're also valuing yourself at a higher level.

As with many things in life, you get what you pay for, and experienced experts are bound to cost a bit more. But regardless of how much you spend and who you hire, an engaging job description will help you find more (and better) applicants.

Ready to write your job description?

Here are six rules to follow:

RULE 1: Your description shouldn't be stiff and dry if your company isn't. The best job descriptions will match your brand voice and appeal to the type of person you're trying to attract.

RULE 2: Talk a little bit about who you are as a company, what you're looking for, and exactly what you need. (You can use your Conquer archetypes as a guide for this!) Because you should be clear about the kind of person who would be a great fit for your company, talk about your team dynamic now, including the tools you use to communicate.

RULE 3: Weave a few critical details into the application process to reveal who read the whole posting and who just skimmed and clicked "Submit Résumé."

For example, at the bottom of most of my job descriptions, I add this: *Please include a cover letter in your application telling me about your strengths and why you feel you'd be a great fit for the team. At the start of the letter, open with a simple Dear Natalie, and in the last line, tell me one crazy, interesting fun fact about you!*

RULE 4: Could this position lead to the possibility of more hours, promotions, or full-time opportunities? Make sure you include that! It's so important that a new hire knows exactly where she fits in the puzzle of your business.

RULE 5: Be clear about the level of help you need. Do you want one person who can dedicate all her time with you? Or are you comfortable working alongside a fellow entrepreneur and being one of several clients?

Whether you have strict expectations for a number of hours spent working on projects and deadlines, or you're more flexible, remember: *How* people want to work is equally as important as the stuff they want to work on.

RULE 6: If the applicant is a creative type, ask for references as well as her portfolio or book. And follow up with those references!

When I was starting out, I made this mistake, and it cost me a whole bunch of time and stress I could have saved if I'd just checked in.

So without further ado, let's put those rules to work!

Fill out each of the following sections, and when you're ready, string them together to create your perfect job description:

PART 1: Provide a short description of your company, what you do, and who you're looking for.

PART 2: Describe the way you want this hire to work, what the day-to-day is like, and your expectations for her.

PART 3: Include the technology she needs to be proficient in. Is there a particular skill set she must have? Make sure you spell it out.

PART 4: Think of a fun little task you want to give to prospective hires, so you can figure out with a quick glance who read the full job description.

Now, take the 30-Day Pledge:

By _____, I pledge to add at least one dream team member to my business team. I know I will attract the perfect candidate for the role.

Holding Your Perfect Interview

Once you've narrowed down your pool of applicants, it's time for the real deal: the interview.

This face-to-face chat (I recommend using Skype or Google Hangouts if you're hiring a virtual team member) will help you pin down exactly who's the perfect fit for your business.

Personally, I tend to keep my interviews pretty casual and friendly. This allows for a low-pressure conversation, and gives me a window into the interviewee's personality. I'm always looking for people who will align with my team and who are aligned in their own lives as well. I want someone on my team who has a strong vision of who she is and where she can contribute her skill set.

Here are the go-to questions I ask in every interview. These questions help me get a clear picture of the person I'm speaking with, her vibe and desires, and whether she resonates with the position we're discussing.

Feel free to use these and then add your own business-specific questions at the bottom.

My Ten Essential Interview Questions

1. What's your definition of success?

2. How do you like to work? Do you enjoy working on multiple things at once or focusing on one task to its completion? How much structure do you like?

3. Describe a person, place, or thing that brings you immense joy.

4. In any given week, what are you working on when you stop, smile, and think, "Wow, this is awesome!"?

5. Outside of work, what do you love to do? Where can I find you on, say, a Sunday afternoon?

6. What would you say your zone of genius is?

7. What are your strengths and weaknesses?

8. What attracted you to this position?

9. What's a project you've done recently that you're crazy proud of?

10. Do you have a job now? What do you like most about it?

Bonus Question: Is there some way you feel you could be contributing a bit more but haven't had a chance?

Now, add your own questions here!

Operation: New Hire

⏱ 1 TO 2 WEEKS

The magic moment's finally arrived.

You've posted the ad. Completed the interviews. And you've Found.Your. Person! Take a minute to celebrate but don't relax *quite* yet, because the final phase of the process involves making your new team member's arrival totally seamless and simple.

This goes beyond training too. There are protocols you have to walk people through to make them feel welcome! For example:

1. I introduce them to the rest of the team, and the people they'll be working directly with. A group call is ideal for this! It's a great way to make sure your newbie feels less intimidated, and ready to hit the ground running.

2. I send over my operations manual and video tutorials that explain in detail how things work. I also give her a heads-up that I'm here to give her any answers she needs concerning current and future projects.

3. After basic training is done, I invite each new hire to send me twenty-five of her biggest questions (usually within the first week of working together). This gives us a chance to fill in any blanks in her understanding, so she's soaring along with her work in no time.

Growing the team is something that most entrepreneurs put off for too long—I know I certainly did! It can be hard to write that first check and most of us feel like we're experts in our field, not experts at hiring and training. We buy into the "It's just easier to do it myself" fallacy and the "Nobody can do it as well as I can" fib. While I'm sure that your tweets are witty and you're great at returning emails, I imagine that you could probably find someone else to do those things *almost* as well as you can. And in this situation *almost* is, in fact, good enough.

If you're still not sure what to delegate, here's a great rule of thumb: If someone can do something 70 percent as well as you—outsource that task.

7

Make a Bigger Picture Plan

Do not go where the path may lead, go instead where there is no path and leave a trail.

— RALPH WALDO EMERSON

STEP 7: MAKE A BIGGER PICTURE PLAN

I believe in soul-stirring meditations *and* tough-love pep talks, vision boards *and* action plans. While most strategic plans are void of all creativity, we are going to take a more heart-centered, visual, and fun approach to setting big goals and achieving them.

If you're an inventive business owner (which I suspect you are, since you're reading this), I doubt your heart is stirred by spreadsheets and bullet points. Thankfully, it's totally, totally possible to create actionable plans, steps, and strategies for your business in a way that resonates with you.

Your Blissful Budget

⏱ 2 HOURS

I hope at this point, a blissful budget feels possible because you have a better understanding of how to read financial statements from Step 4, Get Your Mind on Your Money. For your next mission, I want you to create a budget for the next twelve months if you don't already have one. You can start by doing a brain dump of all the expenses you have, listing them in the space below.

When you're finished, it's time to create your budget in the way that feels most blissful for you. If that's in an Excel worksheet, great. In fact, I have a budget worksheet you can download at shetakesontheworld.com/conquerkitbonuses. If you'd rather use an online tool like Mint, go for it. If you'd rather have your accountant create your budget, give him or her a call. And if you're more likely to stick to a budget if it's written on paper, feel free to do that too. I believe in running your business and managing your money in whatever way feels best for you. What works for some of us doesn't work for others.

Your Bigger Picture Plan

⏱ **3 HOURS**

Sometimes the big goals can be overwhelming. They seem far away and out of reach, but they need to be big so that you are striving toward achieving greatness.

Even when you know these goals are attainable, you can lose motivation and give up because you don't see progress. Most of us need to feel we're moving forward, even if we're taking only baby steps. The good news is that by breaking these goals down into small action steps, you can make steady progress toward your goals.

I start by drawing out five big goals for the year based on my ideal future and active passions. Once I have my five big goals, I write strategic actions and set milestones for each goal. Here's an example:

Goal: Land a guest post for a major magazine or online publication

STRATEGIC MILESTONES AND ACTIONS

☐ From January to June, publish two blog posts each week.

☐ Contact five blogs with a large readership and pitch relevant guest posts.

☐ Build Facebook fan page to a thousand fans to show the magazine there is an existing readership and fan base.

☐ Prepare pitch, including recent blog posts, guest posts, and other writing samples.

☐ Research the names and contact information for editors at major publications and send customized pitch.

From here, I create a checklist to stay on track. I let my strategic actions determine my day-to-day schedule and activities. Now let's move on to creating your Bigger Picture Plan.

This is a key component of your Conquer Kit, so spend some time on this section. In the following pages, you'll outline five Bigger Picture goals you want to accomplish in your business, or your life, over the next twelve months. The only rule is for at least one of your goals to be financially related—for example, an income projection or a product launch with a revenue goal attached to it.

For each goal, you'll be asked to list five milestones to achieve, with completion dates to keep you on track. Below them, you'll create a gorgeous vision board for each Bigger Picture goal. Cut out images or words from magazines or print photos you find online that will help you visualize your life once that goal is realized. Think: What will be different because I realized the goal? How will I feel knowing I accomplished something so important to me? Whose lives have been impacted because I pursued the dream?

BIGGER PICTURE GOAL 1: _____

Strategic Milestones and Actions with Completion Dates

1.

2.

3.

4.

5.

Goal Vision Board

BIGGER PICTURE GOAL 2: _____

Strategic Milestones and Actions with Completion Dates

1.

2.

3.

4.

5.

Goal Vision Board

BIGGER PICTURE GOAL 3: _____

Strategic Milestones and Actions with Completion Dates

1.

2.

3.

4.

5.

Goal Vision Board

BIGGER PICTURE GOAL 4: _____

Strategic Milestones and Actions with Completion Dates

1.

2.

3.

4.

5.

Goal Vision Board

BIGGER PICTURE GOAL 5: _____

Strategic Milestones and Actions with Completion Dates

1.

2.

3.

4.

5.

Goal Vision Board

5×5 Plan

Once I've determined the five big milestones for each of my five Bigger Picture goals, I sum it all up in a one-page 5×5 Plan. Your 5×5 Plan is simply the five milestones for each goal, for a total of twenty-five milestones for a twelve-month period. That means, in any given year, I'm working on twenty-five major things. Doesn't it feel good to think about focusing on twenty-five things, rather than hundreds of to-do items?

I weigh everything against my 5×5 Plan. When any request or opportunity comes across my desk, I turn to my 5×5 Plan and ask myself, "Is this contributing to the twenty-five things I really want to focus on and is it getting me closer to completing one or more of these milestones?" If the answer is no, I usually decline the request or opportunity. The awesome thing about having twenty-five things to focus on is that it leaves a little space for unexpected opportunities and surprises that come your way. If your schedule is jam-packed, you may find yourself overwhelmed if something unexpected comes your way.

Now it's your turn to summarize your Bigger Picture Plan into a 5×5 Plan. When you're done, you might want to tear the page out if you don't think you'll keep this book by your side each day. I highly recommend referring back to *The Conquer Kit* often throughout the year though.

GOALS

MILESTONES

8

Craft Your
Conquer
Calendar

A goal is a dream with a deadline.

– NAPOLEON HILL

STEP 8: CRAFT YOUR CONQUER CALENDAR

It's time to get out the sticky notes and the calendar and open the spreadsheets. We're about to make magic *happen*!

Creating a business you love (and a life to go with it) doesn't just happen. It would be lovely if our dream lives just fell into our laps, but I'm afraid they take a bit more planning than that. And they're a lot more likely to happen if we think about them on a regular basis.

In fact, I think you should give your goals the love they deserve once a month—at least.

In this section, you'll find monthly play sheets for all the important parts of your life—your business and goals, your relationships, your health, and more. We're going to take a good hard look at your habits and decide if they are habits you want to keep, and which tasks you just shouldn't have on your plate anymore. Use this section to plan the next twelve months of your business and life, and look at it often.

Mini Business Retreat

⏱ **2 DAYS**

Finding time to plan out the next year, when you're distracted by the dirty dishes and a full Netflix queue, will prove to be challenging. I'm certainly not immune to distraction, so each quarter I take a mini business retreat. I usually book myself into a hotel, even if it's close to home, and I don't allow myself to connect to the Internet; I come ready with all the printouts and sticky notes I need. I lock myself away from the world and its temptations and spend that time planning my blog content, my product launches, and my big picture stuff for the coming months. It works like a charm!

Your next mission is to plan your own mini business retreat and give yourself the space you need to plan your next steps and get everything on the calendar. It doesn't need to be somewhere far away or expensive. It's just the process of getting outside of your routine and comfort zone and prioritizing your business and dreams.

Map Your Months

⏱ 2 HOURS

Yes, this step is called "Craft Your Conquer Calendar," but the truth is, I have a love-hate relationship with traditional calendars. Here's my issue with them: Calendars can be too rigid for some people. They feel rigid for me, and I'm a type-A Capricorn! I like fluidity in my planning processes.

If you look through the countless calendars available to you today, you'll find they are all the same and haven't changed in years. If we are overhauling business planning to make it more fun and creative in *The Conquer Kit*, we can't leave calendars untouched. That's why in this final exercise of the book I'm giving you an alternative.

Allow me to introduce you to my planning process that I've been joyfully replacing my calendar with:

Month Mapping™

Month Mapping is a way to organize your month in a way that always gives you an eagle-eye view of the things that matter most. It helps you make steady progress toward achieving your Bigger Picture goals, lays out the content you need to create as part of your marketing efforts, and brings everything into perspective with Balanced Ambition goals since I know you started your business for so many reasons beyond the bottom line. Below is an example month, and on the proceeding pages you will find Month Maps for your next twelve months.

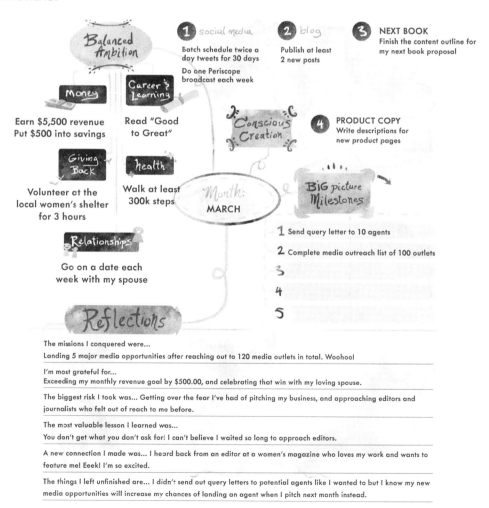

Balanced Ambition

1 social media
Batch schedule twice a day tweets for 30 days
Do one Periscope broadcast each week

2 blog
Publish at least 2 new posts

3 NEXT BOOK
Finish the content outline for my next book proposal

Money

Career & Learning

Conscious Creation

Earn $5,500 revenue
Put $500 into savings

Read "Good to Great"

4 PRODUCT COPY
Write descriptions for new product pages

Giving Back

health

Month: MARCH

BIG picture Milestones

Volunteer at the local women's shelter for 3 hours

Walk at least 300k steps

1 Send query letter to 10 agents

2 Complete media outreach list of 100 outlets

Relationships

3

4

Go on a date each week with my spouse

5

Reflections

The missions I conquered were...
Landing 5 major media opportunities after reaching out to 120 media outlets in total. Woohoo!

I'm most grateful for...
Exceeding my monthly revenue goal by $500.00, and celebrating that win with my loving spouse.

The biggest risk I took was... Getting over the fear I've had of pitching my business, and approaching editors and journalists who felt out of reach to me before.

The most valuable lesson I learned was...
You don't get what you don't ask for! I can't believe I waited so long to approach editors.

A new connection I made was... I heard back from an editor at a women's magazine who loves my work and wants to feature me! Eeek! I'm so excited.

The things I left unfinished are... I didn't send out query letters to potential agents like I wanted to but I know my new media opportunities will increase my chances of landing an agent when I pitch next month instead.

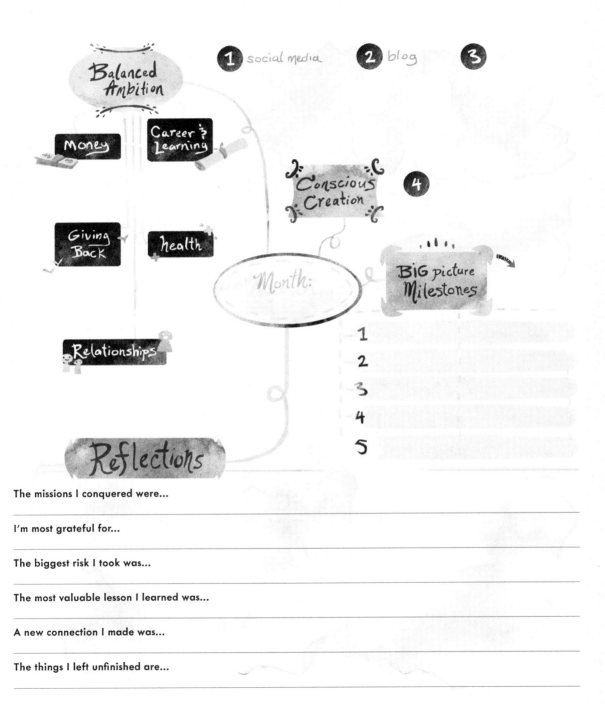

The missions I conquered were...

I'm most grateful for...

The biggest risk I took was...

The most valuable lesson I learned was...

A new connection I made was...

The things I left unfinished are...

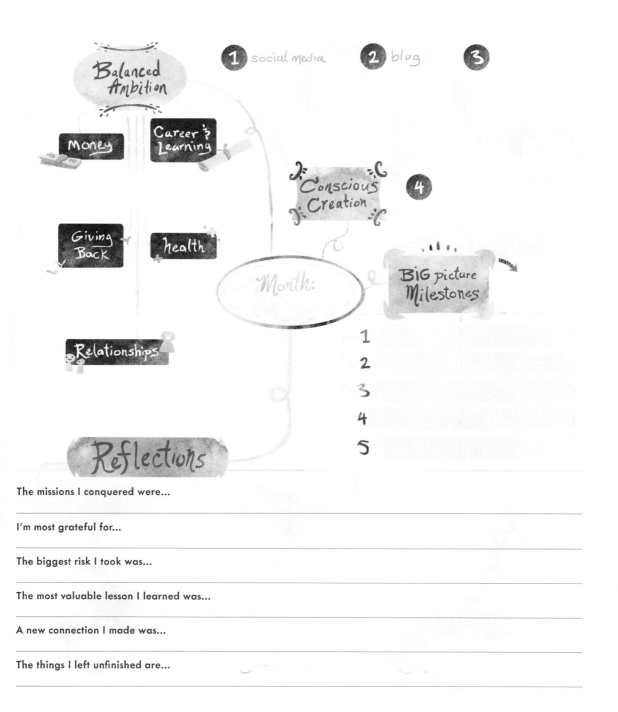

The missions I conquered were...

I'm most grateful for...

The biggest risk I took was...

The most valuable lesson I learned was...

A new connection I made was...

The things I left unfinished are...

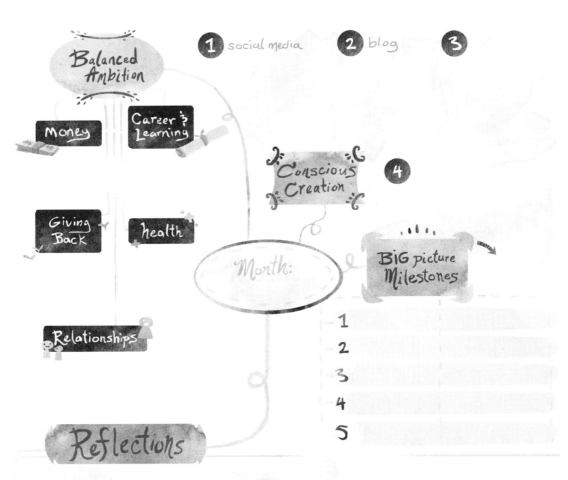

1 social media **2** blog **3**

Balanced Ambition

Money

Career & Learning

Conscious Creation **4**

Giving Back

health

Month:

BIG picture Milestones

Relationships

1
2
3
4
5

Reflections

The missions I conquered were...

_____

I'm most grateful for...

_____

The biggest risk I took was...

_____

The most valuable lesson I learned was...

_____

A new connection I made was...

_____

The things I left unfinished are...

_____

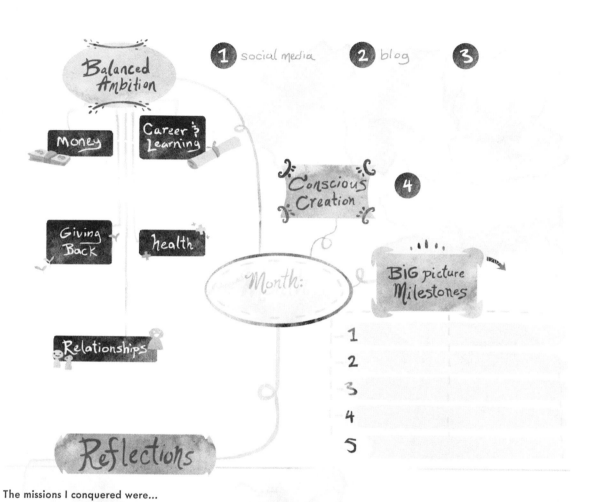

Balanced Ambition

1 social media   **2** blog   **3**

Money

Career & Learning

Conscious Creation   **4**

Giving Back

Health

Month:

BIG picture Milestones

Relationships

1
2
3
4
5

Reflections

The missions I conquered were...

I'm most grateful for...

The biggest risk I took was...

The most valuable lesson I learned was...

A new connection I made was...

The things I left unfinished are...

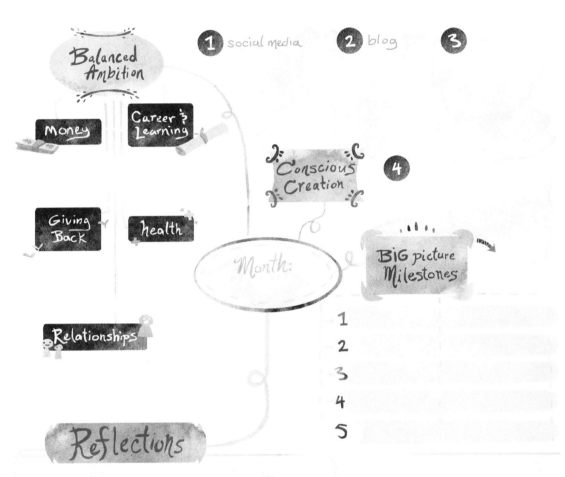

Reflections

The missions I conquered were...

I'm most grateful for...

The biggest risk I took was...

The most valuable lesson I learned was...

A new connection I made was...

The things I left unfinished are...

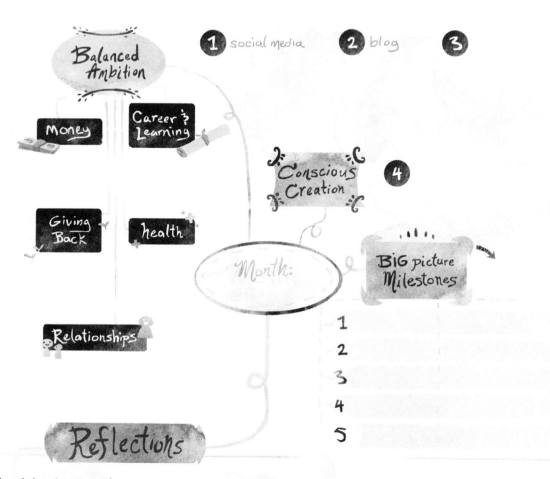

1 social media   **2** blog   **3**

Balanced Ambition

Money

Career & Learning

Conscious Creation **4**

Giving Back

health

Month:

BIG picture Milestones

Relationships

1
2
3
4
5

Reflections

The missions I conquered were...

_____

I'm most grateful for...

_____

The biggest risk I took was...

_____

The most valuable lesson I learned was...

_____

A new connection I made was...

_____

The things I left unfinished are...

_____

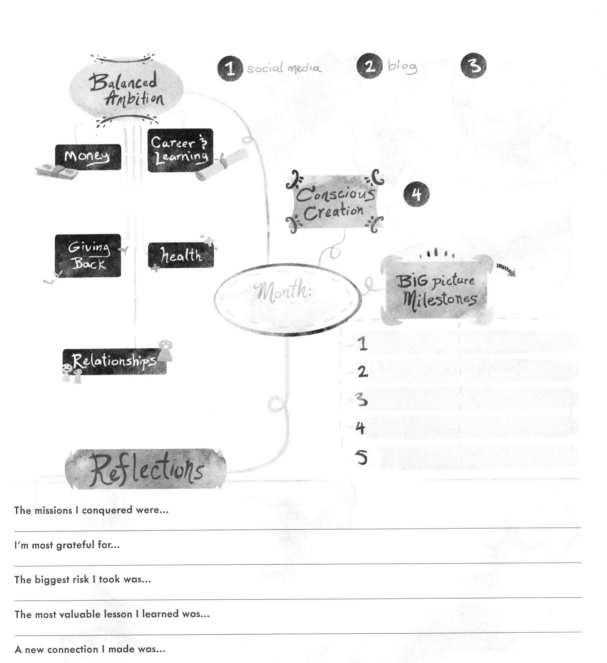

Balanced Ambition

1 social media   2 blog   3

Money

Career & Learning

Conscious Creation   4

Giving Back

Health

Month:

BIG picture Milestones

1
2
3
4
5

Relationships

Reflections

The missions I conquered were...

_____

I'm most grateful for...

_____

The biggest risk I took was...

_____

The most valuable lesson I learned was...

_____

A new connection I made was...

_____

The things I left unfinished are...

_____

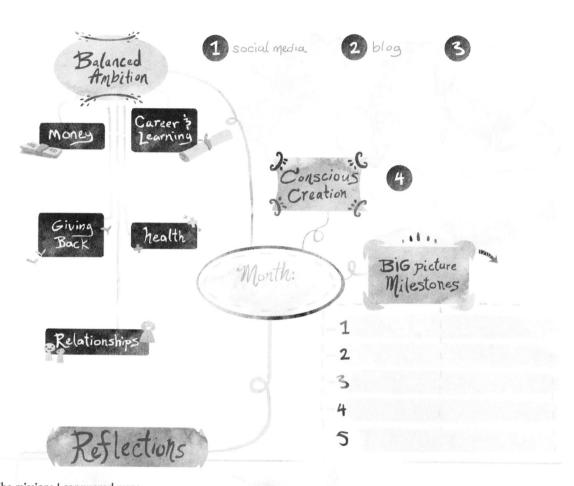

1 social media   2 blog   3

Balanced Ambition

Money

Career & Learning

Conscious Creation   4

Giving Back

health

Month:

BIG picture Milestones

1
2
3
4
5

Relationships

Reflections

The missions I conquered were...

I'm most grateful for...

The biggest risk I took was...

The most valuable lesson I learned was...

A new connection I made was...

The things I left unfinished are...

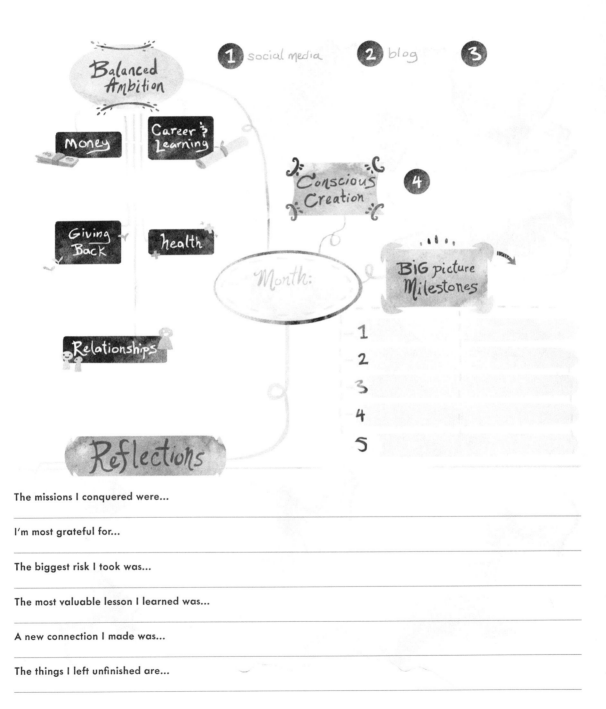

The missions I conquered were...

_____

I'm most grateful for...

_____

The biggest risk I took was...

_____

The most valuable lesson I learned was...

_____

A new connection I made was...

_____

The things I left unfinished are...

_____

1 social media   2 blog   3

Balanced Ambition

Money

Career & Learning

Conscious Creation   4

Giving Back

health

Month:

BIG picture Milestones

Relationships

1
2
3
4
5

Reflections

The missions I conquered were...

I'm most grateful for...

The biggest risk I took was...

The most valuable lesson I learned was...

A new connection I made was...

The things I left unfinished are...

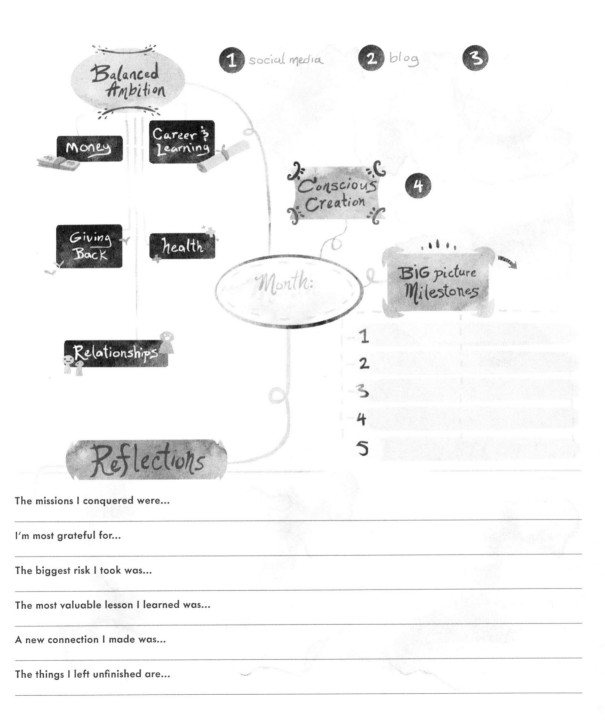

The missions I conquered were…

_____

I'm most grateful for…

_____

The biggest risk I took was…

_____

The most valuable lesson I learned was…

_____

A new connection I made was…

_____

The things I left unfinished are…

_____

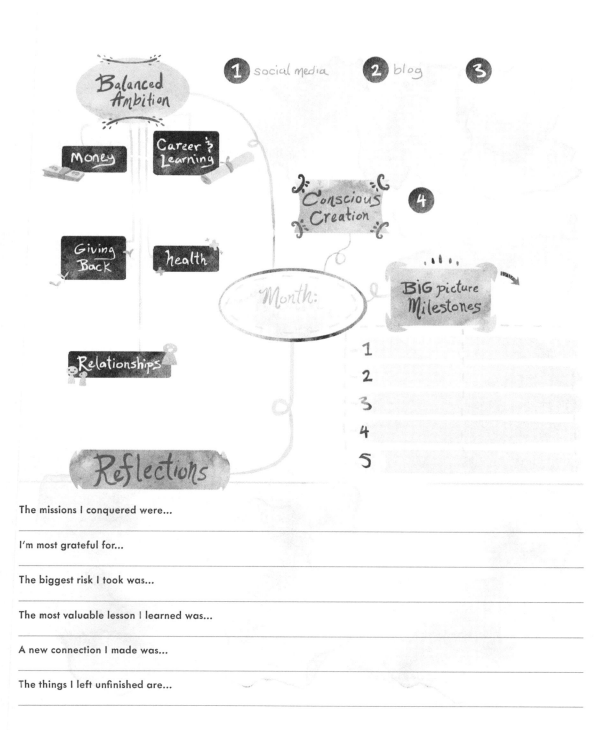

① social media　② blog　③

Balanced Ambition

Money

Career & Learning

Conscious Creation　④

Giving Back

health

Month:

BIG picture Milestones

Relationships

1
2
3
4
5

Reflections

The missions I conquered were...

I'm most grateful for...

The biggest risk I took was...

The most valuable lesson I learned was...

A new connection I made was...

The things I left unfinished are...

Don't you know yet? It is your
Light that lights the world.

– RUMI

You Were Born
to Conquer

As we come to the end of *The Conquer Kit*, I hope you feel aligned with your business and your purpose on the planet in a more powerful way than ever before.

Flip through this gorgeous plan you've created for the next twelve months and share your finished product with me on social media @nataliemacneil. I want to hear all about your big plans so my company, She Takes on the World Inc., can find ways to support you on your entrepreneurial path.

Don't forget to revisit your Conquer Kit and the twelve-month plan you've created. Once you've conquered the next twelve months, you can create a brand-new Conquer Kit and go through the whole process again. It's just as fun the second time, and the third, and fourth. . . . I'm on my fifth Conquer Kit and I love looking back at how far I've come.

I want to remind you that building a business is a long, winding journey. There is no such thing as overnight success, and every step of your journey is a big deal. Be gentle with yourself and your expectations of yourself and your business. We all fall off the wagon, make mistakes, and veer from our intentioned path—it's human nature and it happens to the best of us. You're making things happen and you're turning that idea into something real, tangible, and true.

One of the first times I reconnected to meditation as a young adult was in a monastery I was visiting for a day when I was in China. The monks there looked so happy. I wanted to feel that joy, too, so I sat with them when invited. I didn't last long because I just wasn't training my mind like I do now. There was still a lot of chatter in my head at that point. It was on that day I was told a beautiful Buddhist story that totally shifted my mindset. A traveler came across a wide, rapid river that was blocking his path. The river seemed to go on forever, and he couldn't find a way to cross it to get where he wanted to go. He sat and thought about options for getting across, but each idea seemed impossible. Feeling defeated, he considered turning around, heading back in the direction he knew and giving up on any further exploration. When he got up, he noticed an older gentleman sitting on the other side of the river.

Thinking the elderly gentleman could help him find a way across, he shouted, "Please tell me how to cross these rapids. How on earth did you get to the other side of this river?"

The gentleman looked at him with a smile and said, "You *are* on the other side."

Where you are right now is a special place. Starting a new project, learning new things, giving your ideas the attention they deserve—this is a sacred space. I imagine you've already had some epiphanies and had some shifts while working through this book. Honor those discoveries.

The last exercise I'm going to ask you to do seems deceptively simple: I'm going to ask you to surrender this whole plan. To conquer is to recognize and fill our unique place in the cosmos. That also means recognizing ourselves as part of a larger whole and honoring the fact that we don't have to birth our goals all alone.

Just as we dream and plan and do, I have also found that it has been essential to surrender my most heartfelt goals and deepest desires to a greater power that can orchestrate the goals I want to share with the world.

In *A Return to Love* by Marianne Williamson, she says this about surrendering:

WHEN WE STOP TRYING TO CONTROL EVENTS, THEY FALL INTO A NATURAL ORDER, AN ORDER THAT WORKS. WE'RE AT REST WHILE A

POWER MUCH GREATER THAN OUR OWN TAKES OVER, AND IT DOES A MUCH BETTER JOB THAN WE COULD HAVE DONE. WE LEARN TO TRUST THAT THE POWER THAT HOLDS GALAXIES TOGETHER CAN HANDLE THE CIRCUMSTANCES OF OUR RELATIVELY LITTLE LIVES.

You might be surprised by the outcome when you surrender your goals; it might be beyond what you thought was possible. How you choose to surrender your goal is a personal choice—do what feels right. Turn inward and consider what surrender looks like for you.

I surrender by writing things I want and things I want to release on two pieces of paper. Then, in two little ceremonies, I burn those pieces of paper. I surrender my goals during my daily meditation practice; I visualize writing what I want on helium balloons and releasing each one into the sky. Do whatever feels most authentic to you.

Now it's time to go out and share your light and your talents with the world. You were born for this, so don't let anything stop you. People who conquer don't sit around waiting for a break. They prioritize their dreams so they have the time and space to achieve what they really want. Conquerors say, "Screw permission." "Fuck approval." They cast lines. Spin webs. Chase chance. Hustle.

You can do everything you've planned because everything you'll ever need is within you. You are a powerful light in the world. If you live from an authentic place where your goals serve and positively impact others, you'll always have divine guidance.

As you read these words, I imagine you're buzzing with excitement about your goal. You're imagining the books you'll write, the clients you'll help, the problems you'll solve. And I'm right here, cheering you on from the sidelines.

I will however caution you, dear Conqueror. If you close this book and put this plan in a drawer without taking action on one of your Bigger Picture Goals in the next twenty-four hours, your chance of achieving that goal drops significantly. I don't want that for you, and I know you don't want that for yourself.

I want you to make a conscious decision right now that in the next twenty-four hours you'll take action toward the first milestone you set in this book. What action can you take to move one step forward? Write it on a sticky note and put it where you'll see it constantly for the next twenty-four hours. Go!

Paint the first stroke.

Write the first word.

Take the risk.

Make the call.

Jump out of your comfort zone.

Whatever it is you need to do, do it.

The world is waiting for you to give it what you've got.

THE CONQUEROR'S TOOLKIT

I keep an updated list of my favorite resources for you at shetakesontheworld.com/conquerorstoolkit, so keep that web page bookmarked and check back often. Below are some of the recommended tools that were mentioned in the pages of *The Conquer Kit*:

Adobe Document Cloud eSign

AWeber

Box

Canva

Google Drive

Hootsuite

Infusionsoft

Jing

MailChimp

Mint

Nolo

Ontraport

OurDeal

PicMonkey

Trello

Upwork

Wave Accounting

Xero

GRATITUDE

I was sitting in a café in Berlin, Germany. I was about to get on my first call with literary agent Melissa Flashman from Trident Media Group, and I had butterflies in my stomach. I had a notebook in front of me full of ideas for turning *The Conquer Kit* into a book, including who I wanted to work with on the project. Melissa was listed as my dream agent. Thankfully, she loved the idea. This would not have happened without her, and I am beyond grateful for her guidance, and the support of literary agency Trident Media Group.

I could not have found a better publisher than the Perigee imprint of Penguin Random House. Jeanette, Meg, John, Candace, and the entire team have been a dream to work with. Jeanette pushed this book to be so much better than I could have made it on my own. I extend my deepest gratitude to Perigee for believing in *The Conquer Kit*, and my desire to make business planning so much more intuitive and creative.

Thank you to my creative team, including Marie Poulin, Ami Grant, Hillary Weiss, and Sarah Von Bargen. I can't thank each of you enough for helping bring my vision to life. I could not ask for a better designer and creative partner in everything I do than Marie Poulin. I am grateful for the support of my She Takes on the World Inc. team and family: Julia Jenner, who significantly contributed to preparing the financial section of this book, Jaime Lynch, and Kelly Azevedo.

When I was a kid, I told my family my life motto was going to be "I came, I saw, I conquered." They were a little concerned that I was getting a life motto from a dictator, Julius Caesar, but they have always stood by me as I defined for myself what it means to conquer. I shower endless gratitude upon my family, friends, and my partner, Octavian. You all know how much I love you.

Last, thank YOU, Conqueror, for helping shape a new economy and for courageously pursuing your dreams.

IMAGE CREDITS

This page should be considered an extension of the copyright page.

Interior design by Marie Poulin

Illustrations created by Ami Moore

Image pages 4, 128: iStock.com/Annykos

Image page 21: iStock.com/GelatoPlus

Image pages 36, 201: iStock.com/FrankRamspott

Image page 117: iStock.com/Kuo Chun Hung

Image pages 136–137: iStock.com/amgun

Image "Watercolor design": iStock.com/BerSonnE

Image "watercolor background": iStock.com/Lidiebug

Image "watercolor stains in vector": iStock.com/Katerina_Dmitrieva

ABOUT THE AUTHOR

Natalie MacNeil is an Emmy Award–winning media entrepreneur and the creator of SheTakesOnTheWorld.com. She Takes on the World was recognized by Forbes.com on "Top 10 Websites for Entrepreneurial Women" and was featured by *ForbesWoman* on "Top 100 Websites for Women." She Takes on the World was also honored with "Website of the Year" at the Stevie Awards for Women in Business. Natalie is frequently quoted and interviewed in the media. She has appeared in top media outlets like *Glamour, TIME, People StyleWatch, Inc., Forbes, ForbesWoman, Wall Street Journal,* CNN, *Entrepreneur,* and *Mashable.* She is also the author of *Conquer Your Year: The Ultimate Planner to Get More Done, Grow Your Business, and Achieve Your Dreams,* and *She Takes on the World: A Guide to Being Your Own Boss, Working Happy, and Living on Purpose.*

Image Credit: Hilary Gauld-Camilleri | Hilary Gauld Commercial

Connect with Natalie:

Facebook.com/nataliemacneil

Twitter @nataliemacneil

Periscope @nataliemacneil

YouTube.com/shetakesontheworld

Instagram @nataliemacneil

Snapchat @nataliemacneil